DATE DID WHAT?

BY JILL SINCLAIR

ISBN: 978-1-77084-757-6

10 9 8 7 6 5 4 3 2

Printed in Victoria, BC, Canada

FIRST CHOICE BOOKS

www.firstchoicebooks.ca

Acknowledgements

Gianni, along with being a tall, handsome, sexy piece of man, you are my rock and the one who makes my heart sing and my soul smile (amongst other things, hubba hubba!). You are the man of my dreams and the love of my life. I love you!

Terry and Dino, your friendship and belief in me, gives light to my creativity daily. Thank you for your unconditional love and support. Oh, and your steaks!

PROLOGUE

Remember in your early twenties when it was fun to date? You'd go out on the town with your gaggle of girls and you'd always have a good time. It didn't matter if you found your Mr. Right or your Mr. Right Now; you always had hope. Even if it was *ever* so faint, there was hope.

Friends were always setting you up too and that was good because it was like an extended circle of the people you knew, one big happy family, like those folks in Utah. Well, not exactly like *those* folks, 'cause well, bigamy just doesn't seem like a fun thing (for a woman anyways). But they were happy connections that were good, like a "gooey-cinnamon-bun-on-a-cold-winter-day" good.

Then came your first long-term boyfriend. You thought, No-one has ever loved me like this before, and swooned at the thought of him asking you to, gasp, move in with him. You could hardly contain your squeals when, "Guess what Terry? He asked me to move in with him! We are sooo in love!"

And so it begins.

Those independent times that you used to appreciate become more of a relationship requisite. He doesn't really want to go to the restaurant opening, he has so much to do and he doesn't have the time that everyone else does. *Hmm, I count*

24 hours in my day, how about you? So you continue to be the bold soldier and carry on. People still joke that he's the imaginary boyfriend. Does he really exist? You continue to make up excuses. Then one day, you don't even want him to come out with you. You dread the thought of him actually coming to the art show and making a comment about a mustard stain on the canvas.

And so it ends.

You enjoy your time being single again, 'cause after all, you basically were anyways. You never had a plus one that you could count on, except for your fabulous gay bestie, Terry. Now *he's* married to the man of *his* dreams and you're *their* plus one, the proverbial third wheel that is always sympathetically smiled at when we go to parties. You overhear the whispers: "Oh, she's taking time off dating right now. I think she's really broken," and "She always *was* more comfortable being on her own and partying with the gays anyways." Even some married people could be heard enviously stating, "Her best friends have such fabulous taste and always throw the best parties. She's so lucky."

I just couldn't win at this game, nor did I want to. So this single thing lasted for about three years where I just wanted to be by myself and was in no rush to be in another relationship. Until, one morning I woke up and exclaimed to the Universe, "I'm ready to be in love again. Bring it on!"

All I can say is, I should have been more specific.

And so it began.

This is the story of my Johns. Not *those* kind of Johns.

C'mon now, give me some credit. It's my story of the weird, perilous and sometimes hilarious world of dating after the age of thirty. If you're under thirty, don't *you* worry. You'll still learn plenty on this read. I've gone through these experiences so *you* don't have to.

You're welcome.

Now, as I mentioned, I'm naming them *all* John and assigning them a number. Did you *really* think that I could have remembered all of their names? Not likely.

Buckle up.

John #1

My first date was a set up by a "friend" (and I now use that term loosely). She sent us both photos of each other, but it was kinda hard to tell what he looked like with his sunglasses on and a huge salmon in front of his face. However, I was determined to give every man with a good heart and great conversation a chance.

So, with the "A-Okay" from both of us, she gave him my number and we started chatting on the phone. We got on like a house on fire, laughing and making jokes. Come to think of it, though, I was the one throwing out most of the punch lines. Like a machine gun, *rat-a-tat-tat*, jokes were flying out of my mouth, so much so that I didn't really notice his lack of intelligent input. He was on the receiving end most of my jokes. He just kept on opening himself up to the punch lines and I'm an alpha female! I couldn't help it.

We decided that we'd meet up the next night, and since he was a friend of a friend I agreed that I would bend the rules and let him pick me up at my house. You know the usual rule I'm talking about; you can't let a man know where you live until after the third date. If they're "wack-a-doodle", it usually comes out by then. So, I put on my not-so-subtle CFM booties and my "don't you even think of bending over even a little bit" dress and sashayed my way to the front door when the bell rang.

"Wow, you're tall," he said.

"Nothing gets past you, does it sunshine?" I replied.

Well, those weren't the fireworks I was hoping for. *Oh well,* I thought to myself. *Give him a chance; he's nervous.* He was so nervous in fact, that when he turned around to go down the stairs, he missed the first step and went tumbling into prayer position.

"Are you okay?" I said, as I reached out my hand daintily to pretend to help.

"Yeah, I'm okay. I do this stuff all the time. My knees are permanently scarred with all of the spills I've taken. Hahaha," he laughed proudly.

I rolled my eyes. *Should I fake a sudden illness?*

"Here's your chariot!" he said, as he opened the car door for me.

It's just an Audi buddy, relax. "Uh, thanks," I replied, as I straightjacketed into the car with my too short and ever-so-tight dress. *At least he knows how to be a gentleman.*

I figured I better loosen up a little bit. No-one likes a bitch and we were going to one of my favourite steak places anyways. I loves my meat! So, I started in with my sardonic humour again and we laughed all the way to the restaurant. The valet approached and after John #1 curbed his car and got out, he said, "I'd like to park my baby myself, I don't want anything to happen to her."

Are you freakin' kidding me? Clearly, I was thinking the same thing the valet dude was thinking. "Sir, you're more than welcome to, but you can't park here, you'll have to find your own spot." "He's a professional. He parks cars all day long, I promise you can trust him with your 'chariot'," I said with urgency. We were too close to that steak to deny me that piece of heaven in my mouth ASAP. "Well, if you're sure we can trust him," John #1 said reluctantly, handing the valet his keys.

As I was ushered into the restaurant, the hostess asked if we had reservations. I turned to my date who said, "I made reservations for 7:45 p.m."

"Oh. Well it's only just after 7. Aren't you eager sir?" she said lightheartedly. "I guess he's looking to get the blue plate special tonight, eh?" I winked at her.

"Um, well, can we um...maybe have a seat somewhere and maybe wait for our reservation?" John #1 stammered.

Okay, clearly mama's gonna have to take care of this. "Looks like you have some seats on the patio. That would be lovely if you'd seat us out there please."

"Of course miss. Right this way," she responded.

Efficiency is key people. I have a steak and a beautiful glass of wine or three with my name on it.

Small talk, blah, blah, blah. He knocked over the artisan breadbasket. This was one clumsy dude. A gorgeous older woman came in with her husband; they looked like they were Italian by their style and characteristics. Think: seventy-five-year-old Sophia Loren. Oh wait, Sophia actually *is* that old isn't she?

Well, you get my drift. I made the comment to my date that she was a very beautiful woman and he proceeded to agree and go overboard. Waaay overboard.

"Yeah, she's really hot. Super gorgeous," he said, as he dropped his fork on the ground *again*. The server came over to deliver our meals.

"Hey buddy, look at that lady right there, isn't she smokin'?" John #1 asked our server.

"Uh sir. I would encourage you to look at this beautiful woman right in front of you," the server responded as he slammed down the delicious cow bits in front of John #1. Not one to be the jealous type, and I *really* needed that juicy meat in my belly, so I just dug into my delicious steak.

"Uh sorry, uh, you're beautiful too."

"Hmmm?" I mumbled, the juices of the glorious meat running down my chin. "Oh, don't worry about it," I said, as I flagged down the server for another glass of the wine that was rapidly hitting the Black Card level. The server and I knew what was going on. He was like a kindred spirit as he sympathetically watched my sad date unfold before him.

Another glass in, I suggested the bill and then Einstein told the server that, after his five double Bloody Marys and two glasses of wine, he was just fine to drive. He even went as far as to say that he drove better with a few under his belt. I mouthed the words "two taxis" to the ever-astute server and got up to leave.

"Thank you for the lovely dinner. We are two vastly different people and I can see that this won't work out. Your car keys are at the front desk and will be available for you tomorrow. Isn't that right?" I turned to the server.

"Yes. We have a strict rule of not releasing valet cars to someone who is over the limit. Miss, may I escort you outside to your taxi?" the server asked.

"Why yes, that would be lovely!" I happily replied. On the way past the other table I stopped to say how beautiful and how very in love the older couple looked. They responded very humbly and graciously, saying that they wished me the same joy and everlasting love that they had. I told 'em that was my mission.

I got home, looked at my phone and saw his text.

"So, does that mean you don't want to see me again?"

Let's see…you're extremely clumsy, have no etiquette, are socially inept, and you want to drink and drive? That would be a "no", Drunkleberry-Fin.

GET OUT YOUR GARDENING TOOLS. THERE'S SOME WEEDING TO DO.

"So what's this online dating thing all about?" I asked a girlfriend who had been eternally single.

"Well, I think they're a bunch of little boys who want to play games. I've met what I thought were a few nice guys, but something always changed after about three dates," she responded.

Oh dear god, was she one of the wack-a-doodles I was referring to earlier?

"They just stop phoning. Losers, all of them," she continued.

Hmmm, I needed to consider the source. *She has been single since I met her about fifteen years ago. That's a looong time.* I resolved to check this online thing out when I got home.

From what I had heard from the single lady masses, I thought it best that I try out a paid site. Think about it; if a guy actually has to pay for an online dating service, that *should* mean that he's serious. So, I got myself all signed up and then BAM. It was out of control.

"Hey."

"Hi."

"Wow."

"You look like such a normal lady."

"Yo, gorgeous."

"Your feet must be tired cause you been running through my mind all night."

Uggg. I dug in with my gardening tools and started weeding out the undesirables. I was the kindest online dater, *ever*. I responded to everyone. Okay, not the "Heys" or the "Yos", but pretty much everyone else who wrote me a somewhat thoughtful message that was more than one sentence long. My thinking was that, because they took the time to put themselves out there, I'd want the same respect too.

But, do you know what happens sometimes when you weed out the bad ones? Well, a lot of them feel like you owe them something and proceed to tell you how wrong you are not to respond to them or tell them you don't think you're a match. Well, excuse me *Born to be mild*, I'm born to be wild, so move along and have some class. I can see clearly from your profile name *and* your sleeper of a write-up that we are not going to make a couple. K?

Oh, you live on a farm, are a proud "Redneck", reside a good three or more hours away from me, and you think I want to meet your cows? Um, no.

One dude passed the first level of this online "donkey kong", so we exchanged numbers.

"Hey, I love natural blondes and I can tell that you're natural from your pictures. I only date natural blondes," he said during our first phone call.

Buddy, good thing you're naturally dense and women go hardwood these days or you would never get a date. Conversation over.

Another guy was really engaging and funny with his emails, so I put it out there that we should talk on the phone to see if our vibe continued there.

"I'm kinda busy with things and I really want to get to know you more online first," he replied. *Buddy, we've been exchanging emails for three days. You got no time to hit the phone? Then you got no time to be hittin' this. Next.*

The third email from another dude: "Are you sensual?" *Are there stars in the sky? If you have to ask, you've got no game and you'll need instruction. Move along little boy.*

"Yeah, I've got a condo in Whistler, a place in Maui and a villa in the French Riviera. Why don't you come play?" *My name's not monopoly dude. Stop trying to play me.*

"Thank you for your kind words, but I don't think we're a match," I very nicely responded to a message.

"HOW DO YOU KNOW, YOU HAVEN'T EVEN MET ME YET???"

Oh, believe me buddy, I know.

"C'mon, just give me a chance! I'm a really nice guy. Pleeeeease?" another guy responded to my "No thank you."

Listen, I don't date whiners. Although, I do like wine...

"So, what area of Vancouver do you live in?" I messaged another potential suitor.

"Kitsilano. I just moved back in with my mom, but it's not what it seems. :o) I was fired from my last job and just couldn't quite make ends meet and she still has my old room all set up so it's not bad. It's nice to have home cooked meals and have her clean up after me. What's really cool is my action figures are still all set up. Ooops, TMI? Haha!"

On the contrary, you've given me just enough information to make this decision a whole lot easier. Not a hope in hell buddy.

"I really don't have a problem with a woman who's taller than me," he wrote.

Well, from my experience, if you have to tell me that, then clearly you do. PS: Get some lifts.

Dating tip, if you've got a sexy-ass name like Gianni, don't be putting John on your profile, 'cause guess what, you're John #17 so far. Isn't the point to stand out from the herd?

"So, if you agree to have a date with me, I can make you dinner on Saturday because my roommate won't be home."

Roommate? You're a grown man buddy! If I dated you, it would be like doing the walk of shame every time I had to get up in the middle of the night to pee!

"I know that I'm younger than you (yes, I put my real age online), but I'm REALLY, REALLY mature! I think we probably have a lot in common."

Awww, how sweet. Listen junior, I don't date boys that still have a curfew.

Profile name: "Waiting for someone special".

Well, you're gonna be waiting a looong time with that 70's hair and 'stache combo buddy.

His online pic was in a public washroom. *Keeping it classy I see. So I'm guessing that our first date would be at 7-11?*

Oh, sir you have a lovely smile, but may I make one suggestion? Perhaps you'd get more responses if you put your teeth in. Just sayin'.

After some emailing back and forth with a new prospect, we decided that we might set up a meet.

"Sunday could work. I'll have to see if I can get a dog sitter."

Buddy, it's just a date. We're not eloping!

"Looking for someone who's okay with a beard."

Really? If that's your only prerequisite, it's a sad, sad day online.

"Hey, where's Jack? Haha."

Oh, how original. Like I haven't heard that before.

"I shot him," I replied.

Next.

JOHN #2

"My wife passed away five years ago and, after taking time and healing, I feel that I'm ready to get into the dating scene again. I've got two kids that are the light of my life and it would be amazing to have a nurturing female role model in their lives. I don't play games. I don't even know how to. I'm really just looking for someone to share my life with."

You had me at hello.

So, these emails went on for a couple days, and then progressed to level two, a.k.a phone sex, er, I mean conversation. It was awesome. Every bit of our conversation flowed and there was no shortage of laughter. This guy had me rolling on the floor, and in a non-sexual way! Okay, mostly non-sexual. I love a guy that can make me laugh. It's tiring *always* being the funny one, am I right Amy Schumer?

Third step: we agreed to meet. I chose a place within walking distance because it *is* all about me. I also chose a place where they knew me—maybe not the wisest choice, considering I had a very random date there a month ago that was an off pairing. But hey, it felt like the staff would have my back if I needed it. The chef greeted me as I came in.

"How lovely to see you! Are you meeting some friends?" he asked.

"Actually, I'm here on a date. I'm not sure if he's here yet," I answered as I scanned the room. *Oh, wait a minute. I think that might be him in the dark corner.* I started to head in his direction, as he was immersed in the menu.

"Excuse me sir, your order's here," I said playfully.

He grinned ear to ear. *Be still my heart.* He got up, gave me a big hug and a lingering kiss on my cheek.

"A little spicier than I'm used to but I'll gladly taste," he replied.

Holy smokes. I was full on blushing. Good thing it was dark in there.

We both sat down. He chose to sit beside me rather than across from me and I could feel his knee touching mine. I didn't mind. We got into a deep conversation with major flirting and, as the wine was flowing, I realized that this was one of the best dates I've ever had. He put his hand on mine on the table, leaned into me and said, "I know that my leg has been touching yours since you sat down. I love the raw energy you're giving and I can feel it pulsating through you."

Gulp.

He continued, "I knew that our chemistry was undeniable on the phone and I just knew that meeting you in person would be through the roof. I haven't felt like this in a very long time. You're smart, beautiful, sexy and have such a fabulous sense of humour. I'm excited to see where this goes, this me and you."

I took a sip, no, make that a swig of my wine, and said "Oh." Yup, that's it. "Oh" was all I said. *This* girl's got game eh?

"Oh shit, I hope I haven't shared too much. I just thought that you felt the same way," he said with his big beautiful blue eyes.

"Oh, sorry. I do. I mean, wow, you just say how you feel. I'm not used to this thing you call communication, Tarzan."

He laughed. "See, you're hilarious! Even when you're uncomfortable you have your one-liners." "Well, if I can keep you laughing maybe you'll…" he leaned right in and took my lips in his. Smoldering.

He slowly pulled away and smiled. "See, not too bad for being out of practice for five years eh?" I was in his spell. Wasn't it supposed to be the other way around? I nervously looked to see if any of the staff saw and, with a wink from the chef, yup, sure enough, he saw. *Shit. Oh well, maybe this one will work out and there will be no more random kissing of men and I'll be swapping saliva with this sexy guy from now on.*

The intenseness went on for another couple of hours and then I had to call it a night. I had big meetings in the morning and I really didn't expect the date to go so well. John #2 insisted on walking me home and I "esssplained" to him (yes, I know how to spell, but I was a little tipsy by then) the three-date rule. He said, "Fair enough," but insisted on walking me within a couple blocks of my place. *Okay, sounds good to me you handsome hunk of man.* So we walked, held hands, stopped, smooched and smooched some more. C'mon, when you have that connection you just can't deny it.

Well, a little sooner than I wanted, we were within the stranger-danger zone and I had to bid him adieu. He placed the most sensual, lingering kiss on my lips as he grabbed me close and made me promise to text him when I was home safe. *Mmm, you got it sexy.* When I got inside, I got my "he's a safe distance away in a taxi" courage and sent him a very sultry message. I can't say what 'cause then I would have to start x-rating my books. This tease fest went on until my eyes were drooping and he was home. He said that he would message me the next afternoon.

I was all tingly. This guy was the bomb. Can I still say that in 2016? He was smart, good looking, so funny and super sexy. I was in and out of la-la land all of the next day. Then he messaged me.

"Hey gorgeous, can't even concentrate on work right now. Thinking about you and those long legs of yours."

"Yeah, what about these long legs?"

"I want them wrapped around me."

Oh, shit's getting real here, in the middle of the day even! I cleared my throat. Okay, I know we were just texting, but I had to regain my exposure...I mean composure. "Well, you're just going to have to wait, hunting season isn't open yet." Send. *Nooo! What the hell does that even mean?* Hunting season. What a moron. I nervously stared at my phone to see how he was going to reply, *if* he was going to reply. *Waiting. Waiting. Still waiting. Finally!*

"I only shoot with a camera."

How is this guy not taken? He is so on it! Well, the flirting continued and we decided to have another date. Duh. This time we'd meet where he dropped me off on our first date and then decide where to go from there. *Maybe my place, hubba hubba…*

I was so excited. No, I really mean it. I was more excited than I had been in a very long time. As I was waiting, I saw a car pull up. *Is it him? He took a taxi last time and now it's Friday night and we're sure to have the vino flowing, so he wouldn't be driving, would he?* I saw the car door open and it *was* him. He nervously came towards me and I was confused. Where was that sexy confident man?

"Hey," I said as I waited to follow his lead. He hugged me. That was it. The damn fool just hugged me and stepped back.

"So, where would you like to go?"

I shook my head. *Is this his shy awkward twin? What the hell was going on?* "Why don't we just go to the Louisiana place. It's fun and casual," I replied.

He walked beside me, no touching, no flirting. This was "Twilight Zone" weird. He was a totally different person. We got to the restaurant and I had had about enough of this backwards behavior.

"So, hey. It was hard not to notice that all of the touchy feely you were last time and even the flirtiness that was on the phone isn't happening at all. What's changed?" I asked.

"Oh, nothing. Nothing really. It's just that I had a lot to drink before and now it's just different." That didn't make sense, so I said, "We both had the same amount when we met. I don't understand."

"I actually got to the restaurant about 45 minutes before you and had a few doubles to get my courage up."

Seriously? What the heck was I supposed to say to that?

"It's not that I don't find you attractive, it's just that it seems that I either need alcohol courage or to hide behind my phone and flirt."

"Huh," is all I said, and *this* time I didn't need game.

The waiter came and I said, "No food for me thanks. I'll be leaving."

Listen, when you start with such explosive chemistry and then you pull a fire extinguisher on it, there's no getting it back.

Baby, you are *not* a firework.

And so it ended.

John #3

He was a runner, loved to travel, knew how to dress, (maybe a little too well, I mean he tied his scarf with a fashion knot) worked in finance, was building a new house, knew all of the good restaurants and said he wasn't about the "game". *Fair enough.* So, we met.

He was South Asian, quite tall and lean (from all the running he did), and he was quite charming. He shared about his sister and her kids and how much he loved them, but probably didn't want any of his own. *Good thing, cause this womb is closed buddy.* He was up on current events and gave room for my opinion, so we were able to have some healthy conversations. It went so well that we planned for date two. He wanted to go running with me, so we planned a Saturday run and would go for brunch after. As the week went on, he was a little hit and miss with the messages, but that was okay because we had made the plans for Saturday and maybe he was just taking it slow or was busy with work. He messaged me Friday morning reconfirming the next day and I felt confident that our date was going to go well.

My confidence in the date came to an abrupt halt when he showed up in neon yellow tights with all his junk showing, like a mound of lumpy nuts in spandex. *Ewww.* I know I shouldn't be judgy, but I just don't like guys in tights, especially neon yellow tights. Do you? We started running and were doing a pretty decent clip. Then about a mile in he started to really hoof it. I was straining to keep up, and I'm not a turtle by any means, but this dude runs long distances and was over six feet tall, so he had natural gains on me. I thought that we were supposed to run *together* and chat a wee bit. *I guess not.* Well, I'm not one to whine or to be beaten, so I did my darndest to keep up. Thank goodness we only did 10 km.

So, as we walked to cool off a bit, I was eyeing him sideways to get a better read on him, 'cause I was clearly doing no talking on that winder of a run. He seemed a little more effeminate than I remembered. Actually, he seemed a lot more effeminate. *Hmmm, what's my strategy going to be here?* We got to the restaurant and I saw some of my gays. As we exchanged air kisses, I noticed my date was blushing. *That's weird.* I introduced him and he was actually batting his eyelashes at them. *Hold the phone! Was he gay?*

The host escorted us to our booth and John #3 asked if he could take a moment to gather himself. "Sure," I said, thinking, *What does he need to gather? His nuts are clearly still all there.* He got back to our booth and now everything about him was *screaming* gay. Now, you *know* I have no problem with anyone's sexual orientation. I just have a problem with dating a gay man, 'cause he has *no* interest in my lady bits, except for the occasional motor boating. I started to change the angle of my conversation, honing in on fashion week, designers and fat loss ideas. We were getting along swimmingly and I realized with a smile that, when he decided to come out of the closet, I would love to introduce him to my gaggle of gay friends. It was clear there was no lust connection, so why not help a sista' out?

John #4

He was an older guy that had a huge house in the ski hills by Calgary and wanted to move to Vancouver half-time. He had sold his business, was a wine connoisseur, loved being active, retired early, and enjoyed exploring new experiences. Our phone conversations were always so much fun and he planned on coming to Vancouver to scope out some real estate. I had recently hung up my own real estate license, so I referred him to a dear Realtor friend of mine. By the sounds of the very expensive homes he was looking at, it looked very promising indeed. Even if it didn't work out romantically, I was gonna get one hell of a referral check!

He had initially planned to come in late on a certain day, but in our conversation I had mentioned that I was going to a buddy's yearly pig roast in the early afternoon with a friend, so he changed his plans to arrive earlier for that. It seemed kind of pushy, but he also seemed really sweet and like he knew what he wanted, so I let it be. He drove up because his ex (that he said he was *so* over) still had some of his stuff and he hadn't been to Vancouver for over six months, so he wanted to get it.

So, here I was at this party with my friend and I was getting messages from him. He was arriving at the city limits, getting to the hotel, and then he was coming my way. I must say I was quite excited. He got to the party, made a bee-line for me and planted a big wet one on my lips. *Oh, okay.* He was like a little boy in a candy store, all lively and bubbly and feeding me *and* my gay friend. Clearly he had no issues with being social.

The party ended and we went for a walk. As we were walking, he grabbed my hand. *Oh, okay.* Then he pulled me into a corner and gave me a very passionate kiss. *Mmm.* This was *really* okay now. He was very demonstrative and I liked that! We talked about the homes that he was looking at, I gave him my opinion, and he kept on leaning in for kisses. Then he asked if I would come along with him in two days when he was going to look at houses. *Wow, is this moving really fast or is this guy just super open and easy going?* We carried on into the early evening and, as we gazed deeply into each other's eyes, he kissed my lips ever so gently and longingly. I bid him adieu until the following evening when we were planning to dine together. Oh, I sound so cultured.

He messaged me the next day saying that he was on his way to his ex's to get his stuff and that he would message me after he finished there. Well, about four hours later, I got a text saying that he was confused. *Oh boy, here we go.* I asked him if he'd like to talk about it. He said sure and, if I wanted to come a little earlier to his hotel, we could go for a drink and talk before dinner. *Okay then.*

I got to his hotel, already resigned to what I was going to

hear, and he greeted me with such enthusiasm that I second guessed my initial thoughts.

"So, how did it go when you got your stuff?" I started the conversation.

"Uh, well, it was really weird. I haven't seen her for over six months, but when I got there I felt something," he responded.

"Okay, what did you feel?" I said, feeling an awful lot like Dr. Phil.

"I'm not sure. I came to Vancouver to meet you and to find a place and I really felt good about that, but now I think I need to slow down a little."

"Okay, it was great to meet you," I said as I got up to leave.

"Wait, where are you going?"

"Well, it's clear that *you're* unclear and I don't need to be hanging around with someone who doesn't know what they want. It's cool."

"But…" he looked at me with desperate eyes.

"Look, I'm a big girl. Really, no hard feelings. Go explore what those feelings were with your ex."

"But I'm not sure."

"That's exactly why I don't need to be here."

"Can we just go to dinner at least? I feel bad about this and I really want to spend time with you. C'mon, please? You know I didn't plan for this to happen and I really enjoy your company."

I thought about it for a bit. I really liked the restaurant he made reservations at and I *was* hungry. I'm such a food whore.

"Yeah, okay. A couple rules though."

"Sure, whatever you say," he said enthusiastically.

"No touchy feely. If we aren't dating then this is strictly platonic. No kissing. No romantic conversations. Deal?"

"Deal."

We got to the restaurant and as we got out of the car, he tried to grab my hand.

"Nuh uh mister, you know the rules," I said as I took my hand away.

As we were escorted upstairs to our table, he was touching the small of my back and I was trying to squirm away without looking like I was having a seizure. When we were seated, I had my hand on the table and he reached across to put his hand on mine, but I pulled it away.

"Listen, Romeo, *until* and *if* you get this thing sorted out in your head, there will be nothing romantic," I said with a hint of a smile. This was actually kind of fun, playing hard to get with a man who was obviously wanting me more the less I wanted him. Strange how that works.

Dinner was delicious and the conversation was still enjoyable, but I had made my mind up that this guy was not to be carried over to another date. I said that it was no longer a good idea for me to accompany him on his home search because that was just weird. He objected, but I held my ground. After all, he was in good hands with my Realtor friend.

As we got up to leave, I told him that I'd just take my own cab (thank you) and gave him a hug. I didn't look back as my cab pulled away, but I could feel his eyes following the exhaust trail of my exit.

The Silver lining of it all, or make that, the Platinum lining is: he bought a place in the millions, which meant a big fat referral cheque for me!

Cha-Ching!

John #5

He was very fit and very flirty with his messages and conversations, and I thought; What the heck? We met on a rainy afternoon in a coffee shop—something I didn't normally do because I thought if a guy can't invest in a little more than a coffee in time and dollars, he's not my kind of guy. But, this seemed almost romantic in a way and it was only early afternoon anyways. I sat in the back to await his arrival. He came in, went straight to the back and planted one right on me! I was shocked and a little bit titillated actually.

"I couldn't help it," he said. "With all of the intense flirting we've been doing on the phone, I just had to kiss you."

"Well," I said. "That was pretty bold, but I think I'm okay with it."

Our conversation got really deep really fast and he was talking about his challenges and triumphs in life. He let me know that he was a recovering alcoholic, but he had no judgment on others who drank. *Well, that's good, cause if this goes to a second date, there will be wine passing through my lips.* Our time was short because I had planned to meet a friend for cocktails, so we decided to meet for a second date.

He took me to the same steak place that John #1 took me to and I got a nod from the server that had waited on me before. I wasn't sure if he was nodding in approval of my date or acknowledging that he had my back again if needed. We got seated at the bar waiting for our table and I, of course, ordered a wine while my date ordered a club soda. We chatted and chatted and finally got seated in a big comfy booth. The server came and asked if he could get me another glass of wine.

"Yes, please," I said.

My date was looking down at the table like he was trying to hypnotize it.

"Hello?" I said to bring him out of his eye lock on the wood.

"Oh, hey. So, I'm just wondering, why did you have to order another wine?"

"Um, because I wanted to. You said before that you held no judgment, nor should you by the way, if someone was to drink. Are you having a set back?"

"No. I just don't want to carry a drunk home."

"Don't you worry buddy, the only thing you'll be carrying home is your head hanging low," I said as I got up and left.

Moral: if my profile says I like wine and often go to wine events and you don't drink *and* you have issues, don't waste my time. There is wine to be savoured.

JOHN #6

After a challenging day at work, I really didn't want to cook, so I thought I'd just stop by one of my favourite neighbourhood spots and grab a snack at the bar and a glass of vino. So, I saddled myself up to the bar and was greeted by one of the little cuties who brought me a glass of wine immediately upon arriving. I guess I really *was* a regular. As I took my first sip, I looked to my right and there were a couple of late twenty-something guys with what looked like a late fifty-something guy. They were having a lot of fun and when the one closest to me turned and saw me he said, "Well, hello there gorgeous! What a lovely surprise to have someone so beautiful join us at the bar."

Blush. "Well, thank you," I said.

Right then they all got their orders of steaks, which were placed down mere inches away from me. Damn, my Achilles heel. *Steak.* I had really just wanted one of their fusion rolls, but now I was thinking otherwise.

I guess he saw me making love eyes to his meat so he said, "The steaks here are amazing, you should get one! Hey, why don't you have some of mine?"

The angels started singing. "Oh, no. I couldn't," I tried to say as he summoned the server over to take it to the back and make it into two portions. *Now, how could a girl refuse that?*

So, we got to chatting and even a little flirting when all of a sudden a new glass of wine was presented to me. I looked at dude #1, nothing. I looked at dude #2, nothing. Then I noticed the older dude at the end of the dude line raise his glass to cheers me. *Hmm, okay.* This was a lot of attention for just arriving here. Dude #1 and I got our meals and dug right in. I felt like I was at a frat party or something and I was just rolling with it.

It turned out, upon further investigation, that dude #1 was older dude's son. *Okay, stop right there. This is weird.* And now, as if on cue, the older dude came over. *Was his son his wingman?* We started talking and he really seemed like a nice guy, as much as anyone can tell from just meeting someone. I found out his son was very flirty, but he had a girlfriend and apparently would never step out on her. *Yeah, right.* They asked me to carry on with them at an industry party across the street. I said I shouldn't.

In the blink of an eye it was two in the morning and I was being driven home in a limo. As I was falling into bed, I got a text from dude #1 saying how cool it was to hang out and how he hoped to run into me again. I guess I gave him my number. *Whatever. Zzzz.*

What is making that sound? Holy crap, it's so loud. Oh shit, it's my alarm. Reality was hitting me really early that morning. I took a deeper probe into my phone and saw that I had a text from an area code I didn't recognize right away. *Oh, it's the older dude, a.k.a John #6, who told me he lived half time in a resort town about four hours away and that he spends the other part of the year travelling.*

"It was so lovely to meet you and it would be such a pleasure to take you for dinner this weekend, just you and me."

Hmm, I needed to have a shower, a large cup of java and a long drive to work to think about this one.

I got another text by the time I got into work from John #6 to say that he didn't mean to come across too strong, but that he would really like to get to know me. He said that I was a lady of class and substance. Well, he got *that* right, and *was* nice *and* good looking and he seemed to have his shit together.

"Sure, I'm available on Saturday," I messaged back.

"Great, let's chat a little later and plan where you'd like to go," he texted.

"Sounds good."

I guess I'm either a sucker for punishment or I like a familiar setting. We went to the same steak place that John #1 and #5 took me. We met there and his aura reminded me of a gentleman from years past, like a member of the old school brat pack. He was very bold and commanding, but in a way that made me feel protected. The meal was divine and my date was very attentive. It wasn't a "bang-pop-wow", but it was a "good-nice-pleasant". We agreed on another date.

On the second date, he sent a driver for me and met me

at one of the new hot spots, you know, where all the girls go to smell the food and pound the low calorie vodkas. As he greeted me I felt a little like his arm candy because he was doing some peacocking—not a big deal, but a mental note. We sat down and immediately fell into our roles of Rhett Butler and Scarlett O'Hara. If you don't know who those characters are, then you need to read more.

It was kind of symbiotic really, two people just playing our respective parts. Our night was pleasant, but without friction *or* fireworks—*not that I ever want friction but, hmm, what to do, what to do?* My mind was saying, *He's a relationship guy and is looking for love and doesn't need to worry where his next meal is coming from, or in fact where his next limo is coming from. Do I continue this?*

Next thing I knew I was flying to visit him at his mansion on the lake. He had bought me a plane ticket and ensured me that I would have access to the bedrooms on the top floor in the west wing, so I didn't have to worry about anything becoming physical before I was ready. He picked me up at the airport and, again, there weren't any fireworks, but I thought maybe they *might* get sparked on this trip. We dropped off my bag at his GORGEOUS house and he decided that he'd like to take me to the Crystal Resort for brunch. Sounded good. First though, he needed to stop off at one of his restaurants/bars to talk to one of his employees. I'm guessing his phone was broken? When we got there I asked if he'd like me to wait in the car and he said that no, he'd like me to join him. Turned out, he owned the entire outdoor mall. He stopped in at a couple of his stores and, in the guise of speaking with "his people", took me on a tour behind the scenes. *Yeah, he's showing me he's a provider, I get it, but this is a little too much.* We got to his restaurant and the manager came to greet us, but John #6 said, "This is my *friend* Jill." *That's odd, I mean, I know I'm not his girlfriend. I still don't even know if I want to be his girlfriend, but to introduce me as his 'friend'? Hmm.* He carried on into the back and I told him I'd just wait out front for him. Now, here's the "Are you freakin' kidding me?" part. I got a text from dude #1, his son!

"Hey hottie, been thinking about you since we met. I've decided that my girlfriend just doesn't cut it and I need a real woman."

Right then John #6 came out and we walked towards the car. *Shit, this is weird times two.*

On the almost two hour drive to the resort, we were pretty quiet....

When we got in I excused myself to go to the restroom.

"What the hell buddy? I'm with your dad, on a date! I've got no interest in dating you," I messaged.

John #6's son messaged right back. "But you're so beautiful, confident and sexy. I just really want a chance with you."

Can you imagine what family dinners would be like? This was one twisted episode of Dallas! I got to the restaurant and John #6 was very attentive, as usual, and we continued our light chatting. *Shit, my flight isn't until tomorrow after lunch. I don't know if this mundane conversation can keep my interest and, with all of this other weirdness. Maybe I should just gracefully bow out. There's something about this guy though. Maybe it's the stability, and that he wants to take care of me, that…oh crap. If I have to think about it so much then I should probably tap out.*

Beep. He excused himself to answer his phone.

Great, more time alone to ponder my thoughts.

He came back sooner than I expected. "Great news! I got us seats at the chef's table tonight for a wine pairing series. It's one of the best restaurants in the city and the chef is pulling a big favour for me to get us in. You're going to love it! It's going to be spectacular!" he said.

Now, how am I supposed to say no to that? Wine, chefs' table, glorious food. Who can resist that? Remember, I'm a food whore. *I guess I'm staying until tomorrow.*

"Wow, sounds great!" *Bzzz.* I looked at my phone and it was junior. That little shit just won't give up. I turned my phone off and slid it into my purse. Whatever he messaged me certainly didn't need to be responded to.

I put on my party dress and John #6 said that we'd been invited to come by early to have some bubbles with the owners. *Alrighty then. Bring on the bubbly!* We got there and just as I rounded the corner, there was junior! *Shit, shit, shit! What the hell's he doing here?* He came over and gave his dad a big bear hug and turned to me, "Great to see you again Jill!"

I was stunned. "Hey," was all I managed to say.

"I told dad about this and said that he should get us tickets. I knew he could get us in last minute 'cause he knows the chef. It's gonna be epic!"

I was still stunned. We got over to where the greeting party was and they handed me a flute of champagne. Kind of a small glass for a situation like this, don't you think? I tried to sip it, but ended up throwing it back like it was a shooter. Bless their ever-attentive hearts, they filled it right back up again.

It came time to sit for dinner and it turned out that I was a John #6 and John #6 Junior's "manwich". I was seated smack in the middle of them. Awkward doesn't even begin to describe it.

As the chef and the sommelier were telling us about our first dish, John #6 placed his hand on mine on the table and then all of the sudden, John # 6 Junior (now to be known as JJ) slid his knee over to touch mine. I quickly pulled it away, but a little too awkwardly and I ended up pulling part of the tablecloth with me and my cutlery fell on the floor. *Real smooth.* Now my face was three shades of red and I was trying to focus on the people speaking. I turned to smile weakly at John #6. He was beaming at me like he was the happiest damn fool on the planet. I was pretty sure that look would change if he knew that his son was trying to get with me. I must say though that there was a strange exhilaration about it, a younger version of John #6 with far more energy and vigor trying to seduce me. Two men dueling for the fair maiden's hand. But, what was I thinking? This was wrong, wrong, wrong.

By the second course, John #6 got up to use the restroom. I immediately turned to JJ and told him to back the hell off. Sure it was one thing to be a bit flirty before, but for him to *know* that I was on a date with his dad, to fly here and then have the audacity to be here at the same event and continue this behavior was wrong.

"Okay Jill, I can see that you're really trying with my dad. It's sweet. When you realize he's not your match, I'll be right here, waiting for you," he said with a smile and a wink.

His confidence was kinda hot in a very weird way. I knew this was a game for him, but still, I was more than titillated. However, this was one of the most awkward situations that I'd ever been a part of. *Here comes John #6, and hey, come to think of it, why didn't he tell me that his son would be here and would be joining us?* It was way too awkward to address this right now though. I would wait until later when we were alone. There were subtle brushes against my body throughout the night by JJ and I just resolved to ignore him as best I could. At the end of the night, the driver came to collect us. Oh dear god, I just thought the unthinkable. *Was JJ coming back to the house with us?* My eyes went wide with fear.

"See you tomorrow for brunch son," John #6 said, rather inebriated. I guess I hadn't seen how drunk he was because I was bobbing and weaving away from JJ most of the night.

"You know it pops! I'll see you too Jill. Looking forward to it," he said as he gave my stiff body a hug.

I got all set up in my room and immediately got online to try to change my flight for first thing in the morning. *Shit, they're asking for the security code on the back of the Visa to change my reservations and John #6 paid for my flights.* I needed to hear if he was still awake to try to figure out how I could make this happen. I put my ear to the door. *Holy crap, he's sawing logs and he's quite a snorer! Score! That means that all of the vino he drank is working to my benefit and he's out like a light.*

I had seen him put his wallet on the side table by the kitchen. I tiptoed downstairs and very carefully opened up his wallet. Hey, it wasn't like I was going on the Shopping Channel or anything! I got the security code and started back upstairs. *Shit, it's all silent. Is he awake?* I stood completely frozen for what seemed like an eternity until I heard him sawing logs again. *Whew!* I changed my flight, set my alarm for 6:00 am, arranged for a cab to come at 6:30, and then crashed for a few short hours.

My alarm went off. I splashed water on my face, moisturized, (yes, even in dire situations like this, it's a must) and tiptoed downstairs. I left John #6 a note saying that this just wouldn't work out and thanked him for being a lovely host. I went towards the door. *Crap! There's an alarm and it's on.* He must have activated it from his bedroom last night. *Shit, I can't just set this off. That's not cool.* Just then I got a beep from my phone. My taxi was there. *Crap, crap, crap.* My eyes darted wildly around to see if somehow there was...*hold on.* There was a sticky note on the fridge with the alarm code! *Are you* *freaking kiddin' me? I better buy a lotto ticket.* I keyed it in and presto, I escaped. *I'll be on the plane in the next hour and back to... Bzzz.* Crap, it was him texting me, wondering where I was. *Do I tell him? What if he tries to stop me and comes to the airport. Aaaaarg. Okay, now I'm a *pirate with my vocabulary apparently. Do I tell him the truth or just stay with the note I left him. Bzzz.*

"I'm sorry that you had such a bad time that you had to steal away without properly saying goodbye."

Awww, that wasn't fair. We just didn't have fireworks, there was no spark, and his son stepped all over the bro-son-code and doesn't know boundaries. What if I did date him while JJ was lurking around every corner. Ewww. It was just all wrong. I messaged him back.

"I'm sorry to have hurt you. I really *was* exploring if we had a romantic spark, but I just didn't feel it so I thought it best to leave before you woke up." I really didn't want to bring his son up in this conversation. There was no point.

"Really, well I'm sorry you feel that way. Have a nice life."

I dodged a bullet on that one. I got to the check in and the attendant said, "Short trip. Business?" "Something like that," I replied.

I took a seat and my phone buzzed again. "Hey gorgeous, couldn't stand the heat eh? It's too bad. We could have had a LOT of fun," JJ messaged.

"Stop messaging me," I replied.

"I've got a sweet deal worked out with pops, by means of a LARGE trust fund and he provides very well for me."

Are you kidding me? This kid doesn't know the meaning of "no". Yeah, sure, initially I was a little flattered, but now this was just gross and I wanted no part of it.

Call block.

"Hey, I was abrupt, give me another chance will you. I really like you and I want to spoil you," John #6 messaged.

I don't want to be a manwich. I don't even like mayonnaise. Ewww.

Call block times two.

*Did you know I wrote a book with *pirates in it? Yup, I did. It's called *Pirates, Snakes, Sharks and Miss Fancy.* Just thought you might want another read, lovelies.

JOHN #7

John #7 was *another* business owner, (I really do like that trait, having the gonads to start something from nothing and being successful) loved to work out, loved good food, nice wine (in fact just had a wine room installed – bonus points!), wasn't a knockout in the looks department, but I didn't care. "Stimulate my mind" was what my soul was calling out for. I wanted a good man with a razor sharp wit who could also make me crazy for him sexually.

Was that too much to ask? I think not. A real turn on for me, is confidence and good banter. Anyone who can keep up with me and can throw it back and forth and make me laugh, well, that's better than gin as a panty remover.

He kind of qualified so after several phone calls we decided to meet.

We met at a very classy restaurant. You know the type of place; where even the hookers have to put their cell phones away. He was very excited because he had only eaten there once and was elated that he could get a reservation on such short notice. They sat us in the very romantic corner and he, being a gentleman, gave me the seat facing outwards to the crowd.

Everything was fairly mediocre and I started to sense that I would just eat him up and spit him out. He may have been successful with his business, but clearly he was *not* successful with the ladies. He was trying to keep up, but I still felt like I was the Alpha there. I started to pull back a bit and not be too, oh, I don't know, *Jill,* but it was hard! I couldn't help it and I started back with my zingers. Bam, bam, bam. *What? Hold on.* He was starting to grow a pair. He was bantering back. Holy hell, he was bantering and doing a pretty good job at it. Okay, there were still some warning signs, but I considered this a decent enough date now. *Decent enough for date two? Let's just see how this plays out.* He had ordered another bottle and I had only had a splash (I KNOW, what was wrong with me?), so when I said I needed to get going the server came over, corked it and said, "For the lady, sir?" John #7 replied, "Of course."

We got outside and he got all awkward again. *Sheesh, how about some consistency buddy?* He was humming and hawing and kept saying that he had called the driving service that drives you and your car home. *Yeah, I got it, so?* He then asked if I would like to come with him and the driver to drop me off. "No," I said, "I'm all good."

Then, dude went in for a kiss with his tongue madly flicking like a velociraptor going after the last cheeseburger on earth. I did the full matrix with a backbend previously unknown to my body. I then dodged left, said thanks for dinner, and hailed a taxi.

"Hey, but you didn't let me kiss you," he said, all of the sudden more drunk than I remembered him being.

Now I was grossed out. "No, I'm good thanks," I replied. There had been a small moment in time that it had been fun, but the before and after were library dull.

"What do you mean, you're good? You've said it twice," he slurred.

"As in I don't want a kiss," I replied.

"Oh, haha, I thought you meant that you were a good girl, when you and I both know that you're a naughty little girl who wants it."

Just then my taxi pulled up. I got in and said, "G'night, be well." Where this calmness came from, I don't know. I *had* wanted to say, "Fuck off you pathetic ass-hat," but clearly the nice fairy got ahold of my tongue before I could say that.

I got home and plugged my phone in to see three texts from him: "Look, I'm so sorry. I think I had too much to drink and I didn't mean to be so rude."

"Hey, I know you're there, you just left me standing, humiliated on the sidewalk, how dare you." And the final one, accompanied by a pic of him in his tighty whiteys standing in a bathroom: "C'mon, I'm a stud, how come you don't want to be with me? Why did you take the wine? Do you know how much I paid for that?"

Hmm, I wonder if this catch is still single…

JOHN #8

He was a physiotherapist with his own clinic. *Fabulous! I've got so many aches and pains from overworking my muscles. He'll come in real handy,* I thought to myself. He sounded like he was a good old boy with a sound upbringing, but he had a little bit of a rebel in him too. *Somewhat promising. Dear lawd, let him be the one!*

We met at this very hip and happening place that had long wood and a beautiful restaurant area. We had agreed to meet at the bar to start, by his suggestion. It was kinda weird of him to word it like that, as if to say that, if I passed the test, he would reward me with dinner at a table. Anyways, he was a little nervous, but really sweet. After a bit, he actually turned his bar chair to face me so that our knees kept touching. Again, he was being sugary sweet. He had told me on the phone that, although he lived in the valley, he wanted to buy in the city and was on the look-out for a place. I started talking to him about it; since I used to be a Realtor, I thought I could help, or at the very least help myself to some commission. *Cha-Ching again! Hey, why not?* But, he kind of shut me down, saying that since he owned his own physiotherapy clinic, he couldn't really move because all of his clientele was out in the valley and he would have to start from scratch. *Hmm, why lie then and say that he was going to buy here?* So I asked, "I thought you really wanted a place downtown?"

"Uh, well, that's the hard thing. Since I live way out in the valley, it's really hard to find sophisticated women and I just said that so you'd go out with me," he said sheepishly.

What the hell? He lied. Never cool. But he did make a very good point; I am very sophisticated. No. Focus. He lied. Not cool. "Look, I was in a relationship in the valley for a long time and I will never move back there." *Unless of course, we were only there for a couple months a year, had a place downtown, and were travelling the rest of the year, which was not the case with this guy.* "This is a big show-stopper for me," I said honestly.

He seemed quite dejected. What did he expect? Just don't lie. Don't lie about your height, your age or where you live or are moving to. Not cool.

Oh, and maybe have a breath mint too Stinky mouth.

Next in line.

JOHN #9

He was a city boy at heart, but also had a ranch out in the valley. *Do I chance it?* He loved exotic cars and fine wine too, though. *Yes, I will chance it.*

He was another shorty, but there's more to life than me looking up tall men's noses, so I wanted to see where this might go. We met at one of my neighbourhood restos that had what they call "big wood", meaning a large bar area just like the previous chapter. This was a bit of a swanky place, but I had to know if cowboy really was city material. He came in and he was super cute. He saddled up beside me and we started chatting right away. He was really good at this conversation thing. We drank, chatted, flirted and drank some more. We were getting along like a horse—I mean house—on fire. We started talking a little about our previous lives and I hit verbal pay dirt, as in, he started to spill *way* more and I had to hear it all because it was too juicy for me *not* to hear about.

"About a year after my wife and I split eight years ago, I went to a horse rescue because I had all of this acreage and thought that I could help a horse out with a place to live so it wasn't chopped into horse-burgers. Haha! Just kidding about that last part. Anyways, I got to this place and there was this woman who had brought her friend's horse in and we started talking and she *seemed* so sweet and nice. She wasn't. Fast forward; she moved in with me and then I found out she had two teenagers and they moved in too. The kids had no respect, they didn't help around the ranch at all and I was too busy with my other businesses to really address it. The relationship became sour but I didn't know how to end it and it had been going on for over two years. I realized that we were considered common-law and that she might be entitled to half of everything. I didn't know what to do. I contacted my lawyer and he said I was pretty much hooped unless we came up with a plan; I should ask her to marry me, get her to sign a pre-nup and then everything would be okay."

Was he for real? I thought as I ordered another wine and some popcorn for the show.

"Well, everything was okay at first. We put in all of these iron clad clauses and monitored her and her actions and we had nothing, until one day..." he trailed off.

"What? What happened?" I asked. I could hardly contain myself with this soap opera of deception.

"We had video of her screwing the pool guy. It seemed so cliché, but it really happened. We're still finishing in the courts, but I found out I won't lose it all."

Wow, what does that mean? Is he broke? Is he legally divorced? So many questions, but to abate my curious nature I asked the most obvious one: "So, where is she living?"

"Uh, with me at the ranch."

Are you an imbecile? I wanted to scream. Instead, I just said, "Oh."

"But we totally live our own lives and she's dating again and so am I," he tried to convince me. "Wow, John #9, I didn't really sign up for this. I think there is too much complication in your life for me to be a part of it. It was nice to meet you."

"No. I don't choose this outcome," he said.

"Pardon?" I said, if only to see where the hell this was going.

"I said, I don't choose this outcome. I choose you."

"Um, well, that's gonna be kinda hard, 'cause I don't choose you," I replied.

"But we are destined to be. I had my charts read and you are the woman for me," he said.

What the hell do I say to that? I just wanted to go home— alone—without it becoming a scene. After all this was one of my date places and I didn't want it to be awkward for my future Johns.

"Jill, my goodness, how are you?" the bar manager said as he greeted me with a hug.

"Oh, pretty good thanks," I said.

"I'm so glad that you remembered that we were going to talk about our marketing tonight," he continued.

What? I was confused. *Oh, light bulb moment.* He was giving me an out. *Bless him.* "Yes, of course I remembered! I'm just finishing up with my friend and then I'll be all yours," I said with relief. "Sorry, I wasn't sure how long you'd want for the date, but I told them that I'd speak with them about their marketing platform tonight so I'll have to excuse myself," I said to the cowboy.

"Oh, *that's* a first. I've never had a woman cut a date short for work, but so be it. I'll call you tomorrow sweetie. Here, let me take care of the bill," he said.

Okay, a couple things; no, I'm not your sweetie, I told you I'm not interested and yes, of course you're taking care of the bill. Duh.

This ranchman will be having no part of this little filly. *Call block.* Isn't modern technology wonderful?

John #10

"I live three quarters of the time here and the other part of the time in Calgary for my work. I don't have time to play games, I've been divorced for four years, have no kids, no baggage and I want a woman in my life who is sexy, spontaneous and adventurous." He cut to the chase. *Okay, sounds good to me.*

We met on the beach trail to look at some of the old brigadiers (yes, I feigned interest for about 20 minutes) before we headed on to the market for a beverage. Wine is always such a good buffer. I was in my flat boots, so I was all good to either walk for miles or run for my life. Ah, the choices life gives you. He was interesting enough. Being a doctor of anesthesia, he sounded like he pretty much made his own rules because there weren't many specialists in that area. We walked and talked and finally when we got to the market he suggested he take me for a glass of wine. *Chaaa! Isn't that the whole point?* We got up to the outdoor patio and it was lovely. We began chatting a little more about past dates than I normally do, but I was rolling with it. Suddenly he asked, "Are you on the Sugar Daddy site?"

"I'm sorry, the what?" I replied.

"The Sugar Daddy site. Either you're on there or someone has taken your image and put it up there," he said.

My head was spinning. *What the hell kind of site was that?*

As if to read my mind he said, "I'm sure we've communicated on that site. My profile says that I'm looking for someone who likes to be subservient and likes bondage."

What the hell? "Uh, no. No, that wasn't me. I'm looking for a relationship and not to be a sexual toy," I replied.

"I could swear that was you on the site and then when I saw you on this other dating site, I thought, oh yeah, she's really looking for it."

"Listen, I'm not looking for *it* and now that you've clarified *your* goals, I'm not looking for someone like *you* either. Goodbye," I said as I got up to leave. Damnit, these dates lately were all about my abrupt exit and there was good wine to be had!

Mmm, *wine* is my sedation. I won't be needing *your* services doctor.

JOHN #11

Come here. Go away. Come here. Go away. It didn't start like that, but the pattern kicked in right after the feelings did. Cue Dr. Phil.

We met at a fashion event and I was so not even looking. I mean, c'mon, after the first ten Johns, I felt like I needed a break. It was a pretty packed event and he was with another fella that I knew through being out and about. When we met though, our eyes locked. I saw that we even had the same phone case and we got in the zone, standing closer to hear each other and smelling each other's scents.

"Hey Jill," a woman said as she came in between us.

Damn female. She was asking about business and how she should go about with marketing, blah, blah, blah.

John #11 disappeared into the depths. *Shit.* The night went on and then the lingerie show started.

I got a text. "Hey, it's John #11. We had to leave. [So-and-so] gave me your number and I just wanted to say that it was great to meet you."

Well, that's good that John #11 had the balls to ask our

mutual friend for my number and to message me. "You left too early, the lingerie show is just starting," I said in my boldness.

We bantered back and forth for a bit and then he asked if he could call me tomorrow. *Okay.* The night was looking up, damn female not-with-standing, 'cause she *was* still standing, everywhere I was. *Damn female.*

He had been divorced for about two years, he had twin daughters that were the loves of his life, he semi-retired early (got into the market early and lucked out big time, he said), he knew a lot of the same people I did, and liked fine food and wine. *Day-um, let's get this thing started.*

It was like a whirlwind. We always had such an amazing time. We were laughing, sharing stories, and flirting. It was all so seamless. He was very interested in what I did and wanted to know what made me tick. He made me feel vibrant and like I mattered. I even met his friends on a few occasions (which is usually a sign of relationship progress) and he would very proudly exclaim my virtues (and they weren't 36-24-34). He took me to see the gorgeous house that he was building on the waterfront—and I mean gorgeous! He showed me pictures of the furniture that he had ordered and said this particular two-seater love seat would fit him and me perfectly. *Awww.* The house was all modern lines with a view of the ocean from every room—well, except for the powder room. Who needs to see the sea when you pee anyways?

One night we went to a swinging hot spot and we were

having so much fun. Then one of his best friends showed up and we had even *more* fun if you can believe it. We ended up cabbing it to an awesome new Neapolitan pizza place and his friend commented that we made a great couple—always laughing, having fun and chatting up a storm. He even joked that we should get a room because we were so kissy with each other. *Hmm, I like that.* Now we hadn't talked about being exclusive yet; I just thought that we would work that into a conversation when it was the right time.

Well, apparently I thought it was the right time after we shut a bar down and then went back to his place. My head was booze brave and I started the conversation.

"So, where do you see this going?" *Yeah, I know, not the best opener.*

"Uh, what do you mean? I think we've got a really good thing going."

"Yeah, we do, but do you want us to be exclusive?" I said, unsure of myself.

"Wow, I don't know Jill. We have such a great time together; I guess I didn't really think about putting any labels on it. Look, my wife was my best friend," he said.

Well, clearly you weren't hers because she left you for another man, I thought in my head.

"I'm just not sure that I can replace her like that, especially having my two daughters to consider."

He was obviously still in love with her.

"Can we just sleep on this and maybe talk about it another time?" he asked.

Well, I knew what *that* meant. We went to bed. I woke up in the morning, put on my gym gear and sat on the edge of the bed.

"Look, I don't want to push you into anything, and it seems clear to me that you still have feelings for your ex. Why don't we just let this be for a while," I said to him.

"I like what we have though. But, if you're sure that's what you want," he replied.

I left and did a huge run to sweat out all of the alcohol toxins *and* the feelings that I was having for him. It was clear to me he didn't want a relationship, so I was moving on.

There were a couple of events that week where I ran into him. The first one was a pretty splashy affair and he saw me as soon as he walked in. He came over, said hello and did the "kiss, kiss" thing, and awkwardly went on to meet up with his friends—the ones who I had also met before. I had come with some big-money guys and I guess he was getting jealous or something because he kept on walking past and looking at what was going on. It was quite humorous. *Listen, if you don't want a relationship, don't hover.* Then I got a text.

"Hey, you look beautiful tonight. Too bad you're with those guys."

Why too bad? I thought. I didn't respond. He kept on walking past like clockwork though, keeping his eyes peeled for an opening, I suppose.

I left and went home—alone—for some beauty sleep. I got another text.

"I'm sorry that you left early. It would have been nice to catch up."

Catch up on what? Me having a good time moving on or you doing the stalker walk?

The next event I saw him at was bonkers. Everyone was dressed to the nines and looking to impress. As soon as I walked in he was standing right there. He started walking towards me and extended his arms in a hug. I gave him a side hug and said, "Hey, I'm just meeting some friends. See you around."

"What the hell Jill? Why are you being like this?"

"Well, we both know that you don't want to be in a relationship and I don't want to be a pillow pal, so I'm moving on," I said with a smile.

"Shit, so that's it then," he said as more of a statement.

"Yup, have a great night!"

For the rest of the evening I could feel his eyes on me, watching my every move. I found myself in the family and close friends area that was shut off to the general crowd and when I turned around... "Hey, it looks like you're having a good time. Who are you here with?" he asked.

"I came by myself to meet a friend and have been meeting up with other peeps too. It's been kind of like a reunion of sorts," I replied. I couldn't really move far because there was a slow moving line to congratulate one of the owners, so I was shuffling along as best as I could.

"So, how about we just kind of hang out like we were before?" he asked.

"Well, because in that ill-fated moment when I asked you about an exclusive relationship, you declined and *I'm* inclined not to be someone's option. I need to be someone's priority," I replied. Shuffle, shuffle. The situation was actually kind of funny and I started laughing. Here I was, in a very uncomfortable position, quite literally not able to freely walk away, and I was stuck explaining myself again to John #11.

"Look, it's okay. We're not in the same place. I get it. No hard feelings buddy," I said as I finally broke free of the crowd and made my way to the stairs.

Free at last, free at last! Thank god almighty, I was free at last!

JOHN #12

Now, as if the online dudes weren't enough, I still had well-meaning friends trying to set me up. Thus, John #12. Our photos and bios were exchanged and even though he was about 15 years older than me, we agreed to chat. We hit it off well enough, so we decided to meet for drinks and if *that* went well, go to a football game after, the Lions against the Seahawks. Isn't that kind of rude to stick him with a spare ticket if you don't hit it off, you ask? Nope. Not at all, he's a grown ass man who agreed to it.

We met close enough to my place so that it was convenient for me. You see a pattern here don't you? Anyways, here I was, in one of my favourite places where they treat me like a queen, and in stumbles my bumbling date. *What is it with these clumsy guys?* The bar manager was enlightened as to my situation and agreed to intervene if needed. See, even though he is a friend of a friend, you can't be too sure until you see the whites of their eyes.

"Wow, you're even more beautiful in person!" he exclaimed.

Okay, a point for the dude, but with a minus because of the stumble, so he's still at zero.

He ordered some sparkling water and a scotch. He wanted to be a responsible driver if I were to accompany him to the game because I was "precious cargo". Almost a point, but now I thought he was trying too hard. We started getting into the regular schpeel. *Blah. Blah. Blah? Hey, this guy's actually pretty interesting and he's kinda funny too. Okay, two hours to game time. Do I order papardelle with rabbit ragu or go to the game and have a hot dog? Decisions, decisions.* The manager brought over an appetizer plate on the house. *So sweet of him.*

"I guess you've got some play here eh?" he said.

"What are you talking about?" I replied.

"Nice plate from the chef for us," he says.

"They are lovely and very good people," I said as I dug into the pork three ways. I felt like Gollum; if I was going to have to share it, I was going to get the best bites first, my *precious* bites.

So yes, I decided to go to the game 'cause it was the Seahawks after all! Also, the manager gave me the nod that the guy passed the safety test, so I thought, What the heck. We got out front and his car was right there in all its black, shiny beauty. *Hold on*, I thought as he was opening the door for me. "Is that a pair of tighty whities in the back seat?" I now said out loud.

"Oh shit! Those must have fallen out when I moved my gym bag to the trunk this afternoon." "Reeeeeeally?" I said with my eyebrow raised.

"Yes! I'm sorry about that!" he stammered.

"Are you sure you weren't thinking you're getting lucky later and removing one layer to save time?" I asked.

"God no. No! I swear!"

Hmmm, I can't say that I've ever been in this situation before.

"Seriously, I'm so sorry," he said as he scooped them up and threw them in the trunk.

What the heck. You only live once.

He got lost in the parkade that he *always* parked in, walked into me as I bent over to fix my pant leg on my boot, and yelled at a car that had the right of way. *Keep your eye on the prize girl. You're almost at the game.*

Since we were in stadium seats and not the box, I opted for a beer. Wine is never a good idea from the commoner area. He went to get the beer as I waited in the seats and noticed lots of guys in the area that were big BC fans. My date showed up again and he'd changed his shirt. He was now sporting a Seahawks jersey and we were deep in the ranks of the Lions. *Shit, this might get ugly.*

"Here you go beautiful," he said as he proceeded to spill half the beer all over my boots.

These weren't Hunter boots; they were Mui Mui, so no, they weren't waterproof *or* beerproof. "I'm so sorry! Wow, I'm just not doing well in the impressing department am I?" he said.

No. No you're not Captain Obvious. I smiled weakly and looked at the field willing them to start the game, for the love of god.

When we were approaching half time he put his arm on the back of my seat. I sat forward, signaling ever so subtly, "Don't even think about it buddy." Then a couple came up the stairs.

"John #12!" they said. Okay, they used his real name, but you get that don't you? They carried on with the niceties until he said, "This is my girlfriend, Jill," and put his arm around me.

"No! I'm not your girlfriend," I shouted a little too loudly. But, who was this buffoon to say that I was his girlfriend?

The BC fans were paying attention by now. I guess seeing this odd coupling and seeing my stiff-as-a-board demeanor they thought they would lighten it up.

"Hey, you a fan of the Seahawks too or a BC fan?" one of them asked.

"BC all the way!" I exclaimed. *Friends! At last I have people that I can relate to.*

"Here," another one of them said as he offered me a beer from his tray.

What's the etiquette here? Hmmm. Do I accept? Yup! "Thanks!" I said as I cheersed them.

So we all started chatting it up—even John #12—and the rest of the game wasn't so bad after all.

"You never want to go out with me again do you?" he asked with sad eyes as the fans starting leaving. "I understand. We're pretty different and well, thanks for still being a good sport about it. Sorry again for spilling the beer on you."

"Thanks John #12. It was a very different date, but still

kind of fun. I'll just take a taxi home though. You'll be a great match for someone. Keep your chin up, you ol' sausage!" I said as I punched his shoulder. I immediately regretted saying it.

But if you think about it, ol' sausages need to stick to old buns. My yeast hasn't even fully risen yet!

Feeding Time at the Shark Tank

My girlfriend who hadn't been successful finding love online (yet) pointed out that I must try this other site when she was over visiting me one night. She said that there was this guy that was like James Bond (suave, sophisticated, and worldly) with a little Lenny Kravitz (rock and roll, slim with his own style) thrown in and a pinch of Shakespeare (a way with words). "It's free, so what do you have to lose?" she said as she opened the online site. *Okay, show me the guy.* BAM! He was everything she said and more. *Holy snikey!*

I put up a quick profile and messaged the dude with answers to his fun profile questions.

"Yes, I can run in heels, name that classic rock song whilst choosing the finest of wines, and of course I always have my passport with me for spur of the moment getaways."

Bing. He messaged back right away. "Excellent. You must be new because you're still on here. :o) You clearly have the confidence that is oh, so sexy. Shall we chat?"

Oh crap. This wasn't supposed to work so quickly! My

girlfriend was there and I didn't want to be rude. I looked at her pleadingly.

"Well, what are you waiting for? Sounds like this guy is right up your alley. Call him," she said. *Yes. No. Yes. No.* I didn't want to seem desperate either.

"Tomorrow," I messaged him.

"Sounds good. Have an awesome night," he messaged back.

It was starting to sound like a pinball arcade. *Ding. Ding. Ding. Ding. Ding.* It kept going and going. I was getting all of these messages. I thought weeding through the other site was a lot of work. This was like swimming with the sharks wearing pork chops for a bathing suit.

I finished the visit with my friend and dug in to see who all of these guys were. I stopped counting. It was like a livestock auction, and I was the two legged meat.

I still wanted to keep an open mind so I started responding to some messages. I could see now that this was going to be a full time job. I sure can sympathize with the Bachelorette now. How do you narrow it down when some of these guys had some real potential (on paper anyways)?

The next morning I devised a system: a flow chart. There had to be at least three Mikes, five Daves, two Marks, seven Johns, a couple of Trevours (although one was spelled Trevor, he'd have me know) and a myriad of more original names too.

I felt like Jennifer Lawrence again - *Let the games begin.*

John #13

(not superstitious but...
should have seen the sign)

"Hi, it's John #13. What's doing?" he said.

I've never understood that phrase. Isn't it either what are you doing or how are you doing? So I responded, "Just writing a proposal for a new client. What are you up to?" See? I was asking a *proper* question.

"Just got the munchkins off to daycare and was hoping to meet up."

Well, Mr. Suave didn't waste any time. "I'm busy until about 5:00, so that's not going to work for me. I'd like to know a little more about you first though. Your profile doesn't say what you do with your days?"

"What do you mean?" he asked.

I thought that was a pretty simple question, but I dug deep and asked in a different way: "Well, I'm not a big fan of the question 'What do you do for a living?' so I was just asking what occupies your days? I know you have two little girls, but beyond that I don't know much else about you."

"Ah, well, I have a diverse portfolio. I have a couple companies and some new ventures that I'm scoping out. Whatever I can do to maximize free time. What about you?"

Hmmm, pretty vague. I'm guessing I can do a little more digging if we meet face-to-face. "I'm a communications professional with a focus on brand recognition, community engagement and management."

"Cool! Maybe you can help me with some of my stuff. Listen, I have my Realtor on the other line. Let's plan to meet up tomorrow. How about 6:00 pm?"

"Uh, sure," I said.

"Cool, I'll message you tomorrow."

Was this a speed date call?

"Hey hottie, you still good to meet today?" he texted the next day.

"Sure. Where?" This was kinda exciting, not knowing much about this guy yet. He just seemed so 'on-the-go', even more than me. I couldn't wait to see what he was really all about.

We confirmed where and carried on with our days. Time came for us to meet, so I put my sexy on and headed out the door. At this point, I was pretty sure my neighbours thought I was a prostitute. I was mild-mannered librarian by day and when night came, I was all big hair, stilettos and short skirts.

I got to the establishment first and chose a booth at the back so I could scan the room and see what was going on. Not a control freak at all.

"5 mins," he texted.

I ordered a glass of wine (no surprise there) and waited for my date. The front door opened and in walked what appeared to be my date but looking ten pounds skinnier and ten years older. *Was he a heroin addict?* He saw me and made a beeline towards me. *Shit, I've already ordered my wine, and it's the type of mid-range place where you can order a size, and I supersized it.*

"Hey, hottie! Sorry to keep you waiting. You look amazing."

"Thanks," I responded, thinking that I wished I could have said the same about him. I found out that he had been single for over two years and wasn't really looking to settle down unless it was with the right woman. *Isn't that everyone's goal? The "right one"?*

His eyes kept darting around and he kept sniffing. *Okay, perhaps I was wrong about the heroin. Make that a cocaine addict.* He was so fidgety that he started to make me uncomfortable.

"How about we go back to my place?" he suggested.

"Nah, I think I'll just head home," I said as I thanked the heavens this was over.

"You are so sexy. I was hoping to get me some of that."

Are you freakin' kidding me? "Well, *that* ain't gonna happen Romeo," I said, as I got up to leave. "Suit yourself. I don't go on dates with just *anyone* you know. You showed real promise."

Real promise of what? Becoming your groupie or drug mule? No thanks. Douche.

John #14

An Eastern European. I've never dated someone that was fresh from there. Although, I've dated my fair share of *fresh* men, but this one seemed different. He was an artist. Remember, I was keeping an open mind.

We met at a casual restaurant because it was in the middle of the afternoon and I didn't want any pomp and circumstance. *Whoa, what am I, an English aristocrat?* Anyways, as I entered, I saw him and he was wearing a skintight white running shirt with his gut spilling over his acid wash jeans. *Ewwww.* I needed to escape. *Crap. Crap. Crap.* He saw me before I could exit stage left. I smiled weakly as I approached the table.

"Hi, you must be John #14," I said.

"Yes, and I'm ever so pleased to meet you," he replied with a toothy smile. That toothy smile is never as cute when you don't really like someone, is it? He just looked macabre, like a doll possessed. "Did you look at my website for my paintings?" he asked.

"Uh, yes. I did. Amazing work!" I replied. It really was beautiful and that was half of the reason I had agreed to meet.

"Hi! I'm Britney. I'm your server tonight. Can I get you something to drink?"

Dear god in heaven, you do answer prayers. "I'll have a 9 oz red please and keep an eye if it goes below half." *Oh shit, I said that out loud.* My date and I gave each other those beauty pageant smiles.

"So, you liked my paintings," he said with a glimmer of hope.

"Yeah, you have some talent there. Where are you showing?" I asked.

"Mostly out of my basement suite," he replied.

Hold on. I thought I had learned my lesson and asked what his living situation was already. He had said he owned a house. "Oh, I thought you were in your own house." I queried.

"No, I can't afford that. I bought a place out in the boonies and I rent that out to some bikers. I live in a basement suite and paint houses for a living," he said.

Well shit. I guess I needed to probe even *deeper* when I asked those questions initially, didn't I? When he said that he was an artist and painted for a living I kinda thought...well, what would *you* think?

"Here's your wine! Hey, I love your shoes, where did you get them?" Britney exclaimed like we were new BFF's, which was okay by me. We went on and on about fashion and food until her manager came and asked her to help out at another table. *Bastard, just when we were getting into the good stuff.* My date and I were then forced to chat, so we talked around subjects and weren't making any headway when he said, "I'll never have a chance with you will I?"

Oh, I guess I really am being obvious. "Um, not really. You seem like a really nice guy, but I don't think this will work out. It was really nice meeting you though," I said with that beauty pageant smile pasted back on my face.

I did, however, make a friend for life with Britney. Free shooters anytime I come back! And to think, I don't even do shooters. Bless her young heart.

Is Seven Dates In One Day Even Possible?

This was going against everything in my being, but for some reason I had agreed to seven dates in one day.

Here goes nothing.

Date 1 – Breakfast at the "hip" coffee shop *exactly* on the corner of "this" street and "that" street. Waiting. Waiting. Oh. Text: "Can't find it." Damn fool didn't tell me he was blind.

Date 2 – Brunch at the new upscale bistro. He came in dressed in yoga wear. *Uh, no.*

Date 3 – Coffee. Okay, before I got there I had a mimosa at another restaurant because this was hard work people! And thank God for that because I came into "I've got five kids with three different mothers. Did I mention that before?"

Date 4 – Lunch. "Tough morning in the OR. Being a doctor is quite stressful you know. Do you like S&M?"

Date 5 – Cocktails. Okay, now I really needed an official drink, because it was finally an acceptable time, so make it a big one. "Being an accountant and very shy, my counsellor told me that I needed to get out of my shell and date those I would never date in real life." *Cricket...Cricket...*

Date 6 – More Cocktails. "My ex-wife is still very much a part of my life. She's my partner in business and we still take family vacations together. It's great." *I wonder if she and I could swap clothes while we're on vacation together? Maybe even have a fun pillow fight...*

Date 7 – For the love of god. More Cocktails. I was back at the same place where they treated me like a queen, so I had *that* going for me. Now, this guy I had spoken to more than the others. He walked in and everything else went silent. It's not like the angels were singing, but it was a far cry from the previous duds of the day.

He walked in like he belonged.

JOHN #15

His smile could launch ships. Wait a minute, wasn't that supposed to be a female thing? Anyways, he came in and wow. Just wow. The bar staff and I stopped our little chatter and gave him the platform that he deserved.

"Hi gorgeous, so nice to finally meet you. You are looking ravishing."

I looked at the bar manager in disbelief. Was this guy a gooder? Time would tell.

We started talking, flirting, drinking, getting the bar manager to mix us up his house-made concoctions and we were vibing. *Is this 2016 lingo now? Okay, "lingo" probably isn't right either.*

John #15 and I were reading the same mail, eating the same pizza and licking the same popsicle. Okay, that just got weird. Just know that we were in it.

It was time to get the bill, which he paid for, of course, and we walked outside.

"John #15, you rally shouldn't dwive, you gettin' a taxi?" I said, more than a bit inebriated.

"Good idea. What about you?" he asked.

"Oh, I'm god, no, I mean, I'm good. I can walk."

"I don't think it's safe. Let me walk you home."

Stranger-danger, stranger-danger. No. I can't let him. He started walking me. We kissed. *Oooh, that was nice.* We kissed some more. *Even nicer.* We were standing in a shop's storefront giving each other tongue lessons and I was one horny mofo. This needed to stop. I abruptly pulled away.

"Hey babe, you okay?" he asked.

"Yeah, that's the problem. I'm too okay, even better than okay, and I need to go."

"Whatever you need babe. I just need to know you're safe," he said.

"Oh, I be safe." Apparently I had become Yoda for a moment. "G'by," I finished, as I teetered off to my home.

"Good morning gorgeous! If you want to know more about the man you were kissing last night, here are my business websites," he emailed me.

Shit. I *knew* he had a few businesses but I totally forgot what they were. Good refresher. *This guy just might be a keeper.* Did I hear that he was Jewish? What the hell, I could convert right? I could see myself doing the…*wait, what do Jewish people do?*

We decided on another date. Let's be serious, people. After he sent me those links, I researched the shit out of him and his businesses and it looked good, *real* good. For the next date he wanted to cook me a rack of lamb at his place overlooking the city and waterfront. *Okay, if you must John #15.*

I got to his posh penthouse (yes, I *had* to say it, "penthouse". You need to have a visual) and the view was spectacular, almost orgasmic! Hey, I said "almost". We talked more and I found out that he really *was* that guy from the other night. *Cool.*

He served dinner. *Fuck. You've got to be kidding me. Are you a Michelin trained chef?* I felt like my panties were going to come off right there and then. *I mean c'mon, this amazing food with exquisite wine pairing and the conversation?* He leaned in for a kiss. *Too much. Too much.* I pulled away from him and dug deeper into my lamb, 'cause it was good shit!

"Wow, you really are an eater!" he said as I wiped my mouth. I seemed to do a lot of that. Oh, stop it people. I told you this was not going to be X-rated. This food was like nothing I had ever had. I was in a trance, a food trance.

He turned on some slow grooving classic rock. *Shit, that's another one of my Achilles' heels.* He took my hand and led me to his enormous dance floor (which was really just the space between the movie room and the great room) and we started swaying to the rhythm. Wow, I feel really old describing it like that. Anyways, we started grinding our nether regions together like we were trying to start a fire. Better? I was smoldering. So hot and…wait a minute, that's PG 14.

"I can't. Okay, I can, but I won't. This will not happen, this sex thing," I sputtered.

He started heaving with laughter. He couldn't stop. He was laughing and laughing and then he started snorting. *Hey, that's my thing!* "You are so precious! I have your room made up for you. Don't you worry princess, I've got you taken care of."

Good thing I brought an overnight bag in my car, just in case. Whew, this was hard, this being a responsible adult and all. I hadn't been with someone in forever and as much as I wanted to bone this guy, it just seemed too soon. *Time to sleep. Zzzz.*

Is that coffee in my nostrils? Oh, sweet nectar of the gods, please say it's true. He had set up my bedside table with coffee and turkey bacon (remember he's Jewish). *Oh. My. Gosh. So thoughtful!* I had told him last night that I LOVED meat. I wasn't sure if it had clicked. Clearly, it had.

I proceeded to fill my face with my protein bounty when I heard a faint knock on the door. *Shit.* I hadn't even washed my face from my crusty bits yet.

"Hello?" I said weakly.

"Hey babe, I'm coming in," he said as he bolted through the door and caught the cooked meat still sticking out of my mouth.

"Hey," I managed.

"You're even more beautiful in the morning," he said.

Okay, is he on crack or something? After all the champagne and wine I had had last night, the 3:00 am bedtime, and the lack of any water in my system, I believed I looked like a sack of shit. He sat down beside me and stroked my hair. *Ewww. Even I don't want to be with me right now.*

"Hey, how 'bout I finish up here and then jump in the shower and then we can connect," I tried to reason.

"Oh, baby you look so delicious."

Yikes. I didn't know that I was on the menu right now. "No. We had an agreement mister. No sexy sex until I felt comfortable."

"Oh, sorry babe, I don't want you to feel uncomfortable. You are just so damn sexy!" he said in an Austin Powers accent.

Thankfully he got up and left me to my meat. I ate my dead and crispy fried meat until I couldn't put anymore into my pie hole and then went to shower.

Oh, a rain shower. Good god. I didn't think that I liked them because the water just soaks you like a drowned rat, but now I had learned the angle. When you find the angle, it's almost like your partner finding your g-spot. It's heaven. I must have been in there for almost an hour. My skin was prune-like and I was sweating, but I felt good. I got dressed into my sexy little brunch outfit and came out to meet him on his sun porch. Yes, he had a sun porch. He had a glorious flute of champagne for me and, with a kiss to my forehead, said it would only take but a moment to whip up an egg white, mushroom and truffle omelet. Was he in my head? This was crazy! That was *exactly* what I loved to eat. *How could he know?* I wasn't sure if I could put anymore in my belly after that bacon fix though.

He came back out and placed his breakfast offering before me. My eyes looked up at him longingly. He took my lips in his and said, "You told me the other night you hate egg yolks, you love mushrooms and you would gladly spread truffle oil over you entire body, so I thought you might fancy this."

Well shit, you got me now mister.

The rest of the date was sunshine, rainbows and unicorns. We talked about art, travel, music, food, and it just flowed. I was in bliss, but then I remembered I had to pick up my friend from the airport. *Crap!* We cuddled on the couch looking at the magical view for a little bit longer, then said goodbye. He texted me when I got to my car.

"What an amazing time I had with you. I look forward to continuing to explore the beauty and depth that is Jill. I can't wait to cook for you again!"

Good thing I was already sitting because my legs were mush. This guy, I tell ya. He was making me fall for him...or his food. Time would tell.

He messaged me that night to say that he was thinking about me and was deciding what to cook for me the next time. *Swoon.* We agreed to meet the following evening, but I had also invited him to a new furniture and design company's opening first before dinner. You know my rules; since it was the third date, I told him that he could pick me up and he got there right on time. I liked that. I got in the car and we kissed, but he didn't look so good.

"Hey, is everything okay?"

"It's my gout," he replied.

Gout, I thought. *Isn't that for old coal miners who have bad circulation, drink hard whiskey and chew tobacco?* But instead I said, "Oh, that's not good. How long have you had it?"

"Too many years. It's a pain in the ass, or more appropriately the foot. So I won't be able to walk much."

Hmm, I've never dated someone with any health issues before. Should I be concerned?

We got to the opening, slowly but surely, and it was a huge space. There were four floors of artwork and designs were everywhere, even on the massive staircases. *Uh oh. He probably won't want to walk up those. I know, let's head for the wine table.* There were chairs there to park him at while I took a lil' look-see.

"I shouldn't drink wine while I have this, but here's a glass for you," he said as he passed me some wine.

Still the gentleman, even though he's a hobble along. Nice. I took a quick gander upstairs and came back down to see how my sickie was doing. There were quite a few people I knew, including a woman who ran one of the matchmaking services that had tried to set me up a couple times. Oh, I haven't told you about those dates yet have I? Stay tuned; they're in the next chapter. *Oy vey.* She asked me what I'd been doing lately and I pointed to John #15 and said, "I'm looking to do *him* later." We all laughed awkwardly.

We got back to his place and I wasn't really sure how this whole gout thing worked, but I was feeling frisky as he was doing his chef thing in his kitchen.

"How are you feeling?" I asked.

"Not too bad. It's okay as long as I don't have to move around much."

"Do you want some help?"

"No babe, stay put. I'm good. How's your wine? Do you need a refresh?"

I *always* need a refresh. "Yes please!"

This meal was homemade pasta with jumbo prawns and it was delish! His culinary skills were out of this world. After our dinner we cuddled on the couch and started a pretty heavy petting session. I was getting very aroused and went to move my foot.

"Ouch!" he said, as I kicked his foot.

Shit! "I'm so sorry! Oh my gosh, I didn't mean to."

"It's okay babe."

"Maybe we should just get you to bed and no more of this playtime, okay?" I asked.

"I'll be alright," he said.

"Well, I don't trust *me* not hurting you again. How about we take a rain check, okay? Let's wait until you're feeling better. I'll head home and we can catch up on the weekend."

"You're probably right. Let me call you a taxi and put it on my account."

We talked on the phone and messaged back and forth the rest of the week and then planned for another dinner at his house. *Hmm, come to think of it, this was a little strange, always going to his place for dinner.* Oh well, he was one hell of a chef. What did I care if we weren't going out to a restaurant? I thought we would take it to the next level anyways (hubba hubba) that night.

He said he was feeling better, so what better way to light that spark than to just throw a trench coat on and head over? Only problem was, he called me on my way over and asked me to get some fresh garlic. *Hmm, I'm kinda naked under this coat. This may be problematic. Too bad they don't have a drive through vegetable place, like a McProduce or something.* I stopped at the store and got out when all of a sudden a huge gust of wind lifted up the front of my coat. *Iiiiieeeeeyah!* This was definitely *not* a Marilyn Monroe moment. There was an old guy standing there—poor thing. He got way more than a bag of apples on *his* trip to the grocery store.

I showed up and once I got to his door, I was second-guessing this move. It was pretty bold, and I didn't want him to think less of me. He opened the door and gave me a big embrace and a smooch and then stood back. All he had on was an apron!

"Follow me babe," he said as he turned around and his bare butt was there in all its glory.

Hey, he stole my thunder! What about me? I felt a little foolish and followed after him with my coat still on.

"Hey, why don't we rid you of that heavy coat?" he said as he came toward me and started to take it off. "Whoa, I mean, holy...wow!"

"I wanted to surprise you," I said.

"Looks like we both had the same thing on our minds babe. You're amazing. Come here."

Scene close.

Now, we dated for a moment in time because, as quickly as it sizzled red-hot, it cooled off, ice cold. He turned out to be a complete homebody (always had one ailment or another) and a crotchety old man in the kitchen. "Don't touch that. No, you don't peel apples like that," etc. I need a vibrant man who wants to run through the fields with me, not pick out his burial plot.

Although, if I was in his will that might entice me...

Now the Matchmaking Lady and the First Bachelor

I got a call from a matchmaking agency saying that they had had their eyes on me for a while. *Okay, kinda creepy.* They had a couple of very wealthy men who were looking for relationships and apparently I would suit either. *Hmm, what's the catch?* They told me that these men had paid good money to meet a potential partner and they quite simply didn't have any suitable female clients to set them up with. I wouldn't have to pay them any fees and they would do all the dirty work. *Perfect.* So, I went in to meet with them and right away they asked if they could send my photo to the first bachelor after they had given me a little run down of who he was. *Uh, sure.*

Since I wasn't given a photo of him, their physical description was all I had to go on when I went to meet him. They told me he was just under six feet tall, an impeccable dresser and was always on time. We were set to meet at an upscale restaurant at the bar. I scanned the bar as I entered and it was hard to tell with the dim light. I also couldn't tell how tall any of these guys were who were sitting down. *Ah.* Bachelor #1 stood up and held his hand out. *Oh, okay.* This was different because in this situation you couldn't talk with them ahead of time, so it was completely like a deaf and blind date. Some would argue dumb too, but that's another subject.

Well, he wasn't just under six feet tall; he was more like 5'9" and I was towering over him in my heels, that made *me* about six feet tall. *Now, that's disappointing that they lied.* He got into the conversation pretty quickly about him and his business and how successful he was. I was glazing over until he started talking about fitness and being active. All of a sudden, it wasn't so bad. I guess initially he was just laying down the old fashioned "I'm the man, I bring home the bacon and I bring home a lot of it" to let me know he was a provider. We ended up getting along so well that we decided to carry on and go to one of the new hotspots (where I happened to know the chef/owner but didn't mention that) for dinner.

Well, shorty and I got there, and it was elbows up. He told me that he'd use his clout to get us a table, then went up to the host and pulled in close. All I could see was the host shaking his head. Meanwhile, I saw chefy and he came over and gave me a big hug and grabbed my hand to follow him to a table. *Ain't life grand?* Shorty seemed a little miffed that I was the one with the connection, but got over it pretty quickly as we dug into an appy plate that chefy had sent over. We started to look at the menu when chefy came up again and said that he would like to surprise us with some special dinners made just for us. *Okay, sounds good to me!* I looked around at the very loud room and noticed some people that I really didn't want to see. I immediately pulled up the menu in front of my face. *I know, not too obvious eh?* Right then I heard a squeal behind me.

"Jiiiiiiiiill!"

Shit, I've been found. "Oh, hey, when did you guys get here?" I asked the party animal dressed like cheap hooker moments before her walk of shame.

"Oh, we've been here since lunch!" she squealed again. "Look who I found Rod! It's Jiiiiiiill!" *Crap.*

"Hey gorgeous! Where've you been hiding? We haven't seen you in forever! C'mon give me a hug!" he said as he literally picked me up off of my chair. Now, remember those itty-bitty skirts I wear? Well, my date had a full-on eyeful of my hiney at that point.

After the undesirables left, the date was going fairly well until he said, "You don't have the usual ugly runners face."

"Um 'scuse me?" I said as I shook my head.

"Well, you know, most runners are all gaunt and look exhausted." He really wasn't helping himself there.

"I think if you're getting a little skinny in the face or wrinkles are showing, give yourself some vitality and get some Botox."

"I've got enough vitality without 'Vitamin B' thanks," I said sarcastically.

"Women need to take pride in how they look and there's no shame in getting some help. I made my ex go to a plastic surgeon and she looks great!"

"And how's *that* relationship working for you?" This guy

just wouldn't shut up about this. "Well, it's getting late and I best be getting home. Thank you for dinner," I said as I folded my napkin.

"What? Already? I thought that we could go to the champagne lounge."

"No thanks, too much champagne causes dry skin and dry skin equals wrinkles. You wouldn't want me to get champagne-face would you?"

Moron.

Now the Matchmaking Lady and the Second Bachelor

Bachelor number two was a widower and was a "young" fifty-six year old. He had been married just over thirty-five years and they had been childhood sweethearts.

"Are you sure he's even ready to date?" I asked the Matchmaker.

"Oh yes, I've been to his house and also met with his counselor and he really wants a woman to share his life with. He wants someone he can take away and who can really enjoy travelling with him." *Okay, I could do that.*

We met close to my place. Was there any doubt? He was a tall, very attractive man and he came in his business suit. *Nice.* He was initially quite shy but he was still quite personable when it came to my "running my mouth" style of conversation. Things went well and we hugged at the end, but I wasn't sure how he felt and we were given strict instructions not to tell each other if we wanted another date until the Matchmaker talked to both of us. It seemed more like a money grab to keep control, if you ask me.

The Matchmaker called me the next day and said that he was head over heels about me. *Seriously? Dude should play poker.* We planned the next date and he wanted to meet for an early dinner closer to his neighborhood. That was fair. So, I put my big girl panties on and headed east. The Matchmaker said it was important for him to know that I was adaptable and could be comfortable in his circles. *Honey, I'm comfortable in any circles, oh, except for Tupperware circles. You can't trust anyone who colour codes their leftover containers.*

Well, he showed up in jeans, a Hawaiian shirt and white athletic shoes. *Magnum P.I. flashback?*

Nooo. They weren't the cool ones you wear with jeans. They were real gym shoes like the ones you see those big Americans wearing on the cruise ships. He seemed like such a nice guy though. Maybe I could look past that. Besides, if he wanted to take someone (i.e. me) around the world travelling, who was I to come between him and his comfortable shoes?

We got into some great conversation and I could see him really loosening up. This was good. Time flew and it was time to go, so we walked out together and his car was right out front. Only, it wasn't just any car; it was a 1984 Cadillac El Dorado (but not the cool classic car kind). This guy really was stuck in the 80's.

"Wow, that's quite an old buggy!" I said.

"Yes, I don't really care about material things too much and I've had this since it was new. I've only had to replace the engine once," he said with a proud smile.

Well, money's not everything and who cares if he doesn't

have a new car, he's still a successful businessman who's kind, handsome and wants to take me travelling around the world! *Fingers crossed.*

For the third date I was invited to his ranch. Yes, I said ranch. Now I know I said I didn't want to date anyone out of the city, but this guy was different. I didn't realize exactly *how* different, but more on that in a bit.

I got there and he had to buzz me into the gate to drive up the long and winding driveway. I was met by an old bloodhound (seriously) who escorted my slowly moving car to the front door. Bachelor number two was standing on the porch with a big smile on his face. Ah, he was obviously in his element on his home turf. We hugged and he brought me into his beautiful sprawling rancher with a master loft.

As I started to look around, he asked if he could take me for a tour. *Sure.* As we ascended to the loft level, I started looking a little closer at all of the pictures. There were so many...*Holy hell! That's his dead wife! In every picture!*

He then took me to her crafts area and it was all as she had left it. I was feeling woozy. This was so weird, but that wasn't all. He opened the door to the master bedroom. He still had ALL HER PERFUMES AND MAKE-UP LAID OUT ON HER VANITY TABLE WITH HER BRUSHES. This guy was *not* over his wife by a long shot. Now, I don't blame him. He was with her for a long time, but still.

"Dad? You up there?" I heard from downstairs. "Oh, that's

my son. He and his wife live here," he told me.

"We'll be right down!" he yelled down to him.

Uh, that would have been another good thing to know. First of all, a shrine to his dead wife, and then finding out his grown son and his wife were living with him? It was a little bit much for one night. Agreed?

"So *you're* Jill. We've heard so much about you," the son said as his cute little country wife joined him.

"Yes, and your names?" I asked.

"Matthew and this is my wife Becky. So nice to meet you. Dad here has been talking non-stop about having you over for dinner. You remind me a lot of my mom, but a younger version."

Shit. Remember in a previous chapter when I said I felt like I was in the Twilight Zone? That was lightweight compared to this.

The rest of the evening got progressively stranger and I couldn't wait to get the heck out of there.

The phone call the next morning with the Matchmaker did not go well. She tried to get out of it by saying that she didn't know anything about the shrine. But remember she had already told me that she'd been to the house, so she *knew* about my likeness to his dead wife and also knew about his shrine to her.

This was *not* my first rodeo and Magnum's not the *only* P.I. here, lady!

Back to the Johns.

John #16

What a sexy English accent he has, I thought when John #16 called me for the first time. He seemed so even keel too, even though he had three teenage kids and was the sole caregiver. Apparently his ex-wife saw them only once a month, so was not a regular participant in their lives. Never thought I'd ever want to be a SMILF, but this guy might make me change my mind.

We met at a restaurant—say it with me now—close to my place so I could just walk there. He was so sweet that he met me downstairs, so I wouldn't have to walk up alone. He was lovely: stylish, but in a rugged way, and he just had a way with words. He made me feel like a woman: a sexy, fierce, wanted woman—and we had only just met for the first time.

This was one to watch out for, I could see. We talked, flirted, and flirted some more. *This guy is gonna be second date material.*

He kept telling me that he loved that I was so confident and sexy and could banter. Apparently, the English like to banter. He talked to the servers like I did and I loved that too. It just made it more interesting to connect with everyone and make it fun. He was very much about being the "Alpha male" and providing for the woman in his life and treating her like a lady. *Okay by me!* He really seemed to go with the flow and that was okay by me too. The date was ending and we both didn't want it to, so he leaned in to consume my lips with his. Oh, the rush of blood (and other fluids) began stirring from inside me and it was intense.

My insides were still stirring all the way home, which was very awkward in the cab. I didn't want to walk home after that; I was too light headed. He messaged me when he got home to tell me what an amazing time he had had and how he couldn't wait to see me again. I fell asleep with a big smile on my face.

"Hey beautiful, I hope that you had a good sleep. I woke up thinking about you, if you know what I mean! ;o) When you get up and about, give me a call," he texted at 6:00 am.

Well, I woke up at 8:00 am and thought I better have a coffee before I got into this flirty banter session. With one coffee down, I called him and just melted with his accent again. *Oh so sexy first thing in the morning.* We planned, or more appropriately, *he* planned our next date. We were going to meet at this fun new resto and then go to see *Heart* in front row seats! *Yeah baby! He might just be getting lucky tonight!*

I met him at the restaurant and he was his usual touchy, sexy, feely self and I was loving it. I just felt so sensual with him. We fed each other—I know, the thing you roll your eyes at when you see that happening at a restaurant—and we were laughing and having a wonderful time. Then when we got to the concert, it was amaze-balls! Front row to see Ann and Nancy kicking it up old school! It was such a fun date.

Now, even though it was only our second date, I agreed to let him drive me home. When we got out front of my place we had a pretty serious make-out session. It was so deep and pulsating, like nothing I'd ever experienced before. I know I've said that before, but it seriously was! I broke away from his lips to say goodbye because I was wanting him sooo bad that I had to jump out of the car. It was either that or jumping on *him* and I don't think my neighbours would have appreciated that. Steamy windows, cries of ecstasy, foot prints on the windshield…

We messaged and bantered for the next couple days until we planned to meet up again and this time he wanted to make me dinner. Now I knew that there was no danger of him becoming a dull homebody like the other John because of his vibrant demeanor, so I wasn't worried about a pattern happening there.

I got to his house and I was greeted by both his daughters. *Oh, um, how lovely.*

"Hello sweetheart!" he said in his sexy accent as he came to embrace me. "Terribly sorry to spring this on you darling, but their mother suddenly couldn't have them this evening."

"Oh, um, not a problem," I was thinking as my sex barometer went plummeting in a downwards spiral.

The girls were thirteen and fourteen and actually turned out to be very sweet—a little clingy, but who could blame them while having such an absentee mother. He fed them first, told them to get busy with their homework, then set to making me a very delicious melt-in-my mouth steak. We had a brilliant night and after the girls went to bed we carried on where we had left off the other day.

Morning came early as I rolled over in the guest room and heard him scurrying his girls off to school. He came into the bedroom with a welcoming cup of coffee and a boner.

"The girls are off and this is technically our third date," he said with a wink.

Haha. This guy was smooth.

Scene close.

I had been invited to a flamboyantly gay couple's party and you *know* I love those parties. I wasn't sure if it was too soon for my date's unveiling though. I've never been one to bring men who aren't "keepers" to my friends' places and I couldn't be sure if this was leading into something long term. It sure seemed like it was. *What the hell?* I invited him and he seemed excited. Although when he kept reiterating the fact that he was an "Alpha male" again, I found that a little strange. But, I just let it be. He said that he didn't have any gay friends and had never spent any time around "gays", but welcomed being introduced to my friends. I told him that friends are friends and their sexual preferences were irrelevant to me, unless of course they were into animals; that's just wrong. He seemed to get it.

The night came for the party. We taxied there and I could feel that he was a little nervous. *No big deal.* He was meeting some of my friends for the first time, so that was reasonable.

"Eeeeeeeeeeeeeeeee!" my friend squealed as I walked in and he came running on his tippy toes towards me. We giggled and embraced and then I introduced him to John #16.

"Oh my, you *are* a handsome devil aren't you?" my friend said as he offered his hand to him. "Thank you," John #16 replied a little awkwardly.

"It's like it's your coming out party, but you're not coming out of 'THE' closet, it's out of Jill's closet!"

John #16 went sheet white. Let's get a drink in him, I thought. We got to the bartender and John #16 got himself a double and me a red wine. We came around the corner and saw a few of my other gays. These friends weren't as flamboyant, so I wanted to see how this would go. I introduced him to them and it seemed to be going along swimmingly. We were all laughing, but John #16 seemed touchier than ever with me. I noticed, though, that it was more of an Alpha male behaviour than him romantically connecting .

It was getting late and the piano sing-a-long was starting, so we decided to leave and go back to his place. I wanted to have a debrief on the way back—as we ladies like to—but he was pretty quiet and that seemed uncharacteristic, so we just carried on mostly in silence all the way back to his place.

The next morning he was very distant and I asked him about

it. He didn't really have an answer, but I somehow knew that this had ended. I left. I didn't call him. I didn't even text him. I just let it go. Something had changed and it wasn't me.

After a couple days, he messaged me and asked if he could call and talk. I said sure. What it came down to, he said, was he really wasn't comfortable being with my gay friends. That wasn't cool with me and he knew that. But there was something else bugging me in the back of my mind. He was *always* talking about how "Alpha" he was and asserting his manliness. Maybe this was a little too close to home. You know, *Et tu, Brute?*

Hmmmm.

JOHN #17

This was a setup from another Matchmaker and I was hoping (for my sake) that she had morals, unlike the other one. With the other matchmaking service there was no contact before the date, but this was a little different. There was a brief "courtship" allowed with one lengthy email from a special matchmaking email account and then *bang*, here we were.

Or at least, here *I* was sitting in the same restaurant I was just at with John #8, but over in the wine room. Clearly, I had already passed the first test, skipped the bar seat, and made it to the table right away. Yes, I'm being cheeky.

I ordered a glass of vino and waited. Now, I know things happen. People can be held up and all, but this was bordering on not cool. I was just about to up and leave when in walks John #17 with a bouquet of flowers and the smell of whiskey emanating from every pore of his being.

"I'm so sorry for keeping you waiting. I was at a golf tournament today and it went a little longer than anticipated," he said.

Huh, that's the first sign of disrespect. He sat down and asked the server for a(nother) drink. "How was your day? You look absolutely beautiful by the way."

Hmm, am I being too judgy? We started talking and I was trying to give him the benefit of the doubt when his phone rang.

"Oh, sorry, I'll just send that to message," he said.

We tried to pick it up where we left off and his phone rang again. Now he said, "I'm sorry, it's my ex-wife calling again. I have to take it," as he got up from the table.

Well, it could be an emergency with his kids or something, I tried to reason in my head.

He came back. "Sorry about that."

"Is everything okay?" I asked.

"Oh yeah. She knows I'm out on a date, but she just had a question about our sons' costume for his superhero party," he replied.

Are you kidding me? He just admitted that she knew he was on a date and yet she still contacted him about a non-emergency subject. Also, the dude seemed okay with it, like it happened all the time. I couldn't just let this lie. "If she knew you were on a date, why would she contact you with something that wasn't an emergency?"

"Oh, she's pretty needy. She's in a new relationship but I guess I'm still the real man in her life." Well, *this* date was over. "Look, I'm not one to come in between a man and his ex and with your situation, I really don't want to be a part of it," I told him.

"Really? You're the second woman to say they don't want to be a part of this. That's just strange," he said.

No sir, you're strange. I couldn't believe in the three years after his divorce only one other woman had the balls to say it. I took my flowers and my dignity, left the table, and immediately went to a drive through. A woman's still gotta eat you know!

John #18

Again, like John #6, #11 and #15, this was a guy who lived with a beach view, but he was also right on the water and owned his own company, had two grown children, and was active. *Let's have a go.*

We met up on a Saturday at about 2:00 pm because I thought, if it went well, we could carry over to dinner. Made sense to me. I was standing at the open market waiting when I saw who I thought was him. I gave a little wave. Guy didn't acknowledge me, so I thought I had the wrong dude. Nope, he circled back and started straining his eyes and as he got closer said, "Ah Jill! So nice to meet you!"

Maybe wear the glasses you've been prescribed buddy. "Hey, nice to meet you too John #18," I responded.

We started walking, as you do on an afternoon date in the market, and he was a little goofy but still fun enough. We decided—and by "we", I mean "me"—that it was time for a glass of wine, so we went to this outdoor patio with a gorgeous view of the water. Clearly, I'm a sucker for a water view! We started chatting away and I noticed something odd about his face. I couldn't quite place it, but something was definitely odd.

We continued talking and the conversation started getting a little off the general topics of restaurants, activities, sports and such. He started talking a lot about women's clothes, make-up and shoes. *Hmmm, okay, that's a little different.* He asked if I had any gay friends and I said yes and told him a little about my dear friends. He then asked if I went to gay dance clubs. I said, "Not so much anymore, you know, kinda over it."

Do I know any cross-dressers?

"Yeah," I said, "I know a few."

"What do you think about them?" he asked.

"I've had some come to my charity events and they're so much fun and such over the top performers."

He then asked if I knew any cross dressers that were heterosexual. *Dear god in heaven! That's it! That's what's different about him.* Some of the cross-dressers and drag queens I knew had this certain complexion to their faces because of all of the heavy make-up they wear. John #18 had that complexion! "Your shoes are gorgeous! What size are they?" he asked as I was finally putting two and two together.

"Uh, size 6, so they won't fit you," I said out loud. *Whoops. I didn't mean to say the last part.* "Haha, oh you silly. I know I can't fit into your clothes or shoes. Good heavens, I'm over six feet tall and my shoes are size 12."

Well, King of Queens, it's been a slice.

So Here's What I've Learned So Far

If you're looking for an "Oprah-ism" from me, you're not going to get it. Do I *look* like a gorgeous black media mogul who's worth billions?

I'm not a bad person for having fun on dates even if I realize 20 minutes in that I'm not interested in them romantically. I give them a shot. Hell, they give me a shot too! If it works for a moment in time, then great. If it doesn't, then there's always wine.

You don't owe anyone anything except good manners and kindness. So, if someone takes you out on a date and says you "owe" them anything (i.e. a kiss, a fondle, a grope, some tongue, or sex), tell 'em to fuck off (unless of course you *want* some of that, cause c'mon, we're all adults here and if you want a little 'sumpin 'sumpin, who am I to say otherwise?).

Never settle. There are always going to be those guys that look good on paper, who will provide well, and generally be nice guys, but don't you wanna be bangin' them well into your old age too? Hot, sexy, sizzle people. You NEED it! If there's no attraction, it ain't never gonna happen. If you want a non-sexual companion, then why are you reading this book about dating? Maybe 'cause it's funny. Okay, you got me there...

Stop accepting negative vibes from your "friends". Throw away what others say when they're all negative. Look at their lives. Is there anything that you remotely want to emulate in your life from them? No? Then stop listening to them. You know you have those friends who play with their poo. The first time they come over and they complain about whatever, they get you to play with their poo 'cause that's what friends do. You empathize and agree that things should change. The next time they come over and start playing with the same piece of poo, it gets uncomfortable. You don't really want to play with it, but you still do. This goes on and on, them coming in with the same shit, never changing it, never flushing it. Stop it now. Take control and tell those negative people who are always complaining about the same thing to FLUSH THEIR SHIT BECAUSE YOU'RE SICK OF IT. Wow, clearly this has been on my mind for a bit.

Talk to strangers. Really, it's fun. At first, it might be really uncomfortable and you might even feel stalker-ish, depending on if this "stranger" is someone you've had your eye on for a while. *Ahem...anyways.* But, you learn, you grow, and sometimes that old dolly at the drug store really just needed to know that she mattered. Trust me. It's great for the soul.

Sometimes life can suck. Now, not in the negative play with your poo kind of way (two paragraphs above), but in the "Man, why the hell did *that* happen?" way. Who *hasn't* been all scrunched up in the fetal position in the corner of their living room? Oh, *you* haven't? Well then, carry on princess. Those of you who have, listen: life can be hard and there aren't any "not fair" chants that can change it. All I know is that being positive and always trying to see the bright side has stopped me from picking a bridge many a time. Your life is what *you* choose. Choose wisely.

Now back to the Johns.

JOHN #19

H ere I was minding my own business at a restaurant opening and this young buck came up, all in my face.

"Hey beautiful, can I buy you a drink?"

*Okay, two things come to mind buddy: drinks are free, and I
don't know "can" you?* So I ignored him.

"Hey beautiful, I'm not *all* that bad."

So you agree that you have some bad.

"I was just trying to be funny and I guess that didn't work.
I'm John #19. I play with "John's" hockey team," he said (c'mon,
you know I can't kiss and tell).

I stared blankly at him. Okay, now I noticed, as I was staring at him, he was pretty darn cute. I still said nothing though.

"Hey, can you just give me a chance please? I just want to
talk to you," he said, just as a friend came up and said, "Jill,
I see you've met John #19. He plays for John's hockey team."

Thanks for giving him my name dude.

"Yes, he told me. You know me, though. I'm not really into
sports *players*."

"Ooo, that's harsh sweetness. What happened to you to
turn you away from guys who play sports?"

"Overpaid wankers who play for part of a year," I offered.

"Wow, you really aren't going to give me a fair shake are you?"

"Probably not," I said as my friend abruptly left the hostile environment.

This banter went on for a while and I was actually impressed that this young buck was going toe-to-toe with me. We continued on throughout the evening and I started to take a shine to him, just a little. A bunch of us went out for a little nightcap and junior stuck right by my side even though there were twenty-somethings with napkins for dresses and inflatables for breasts. I was a little more impressed, unless this was a bet thing. *In that case, I will rip out his testicles one by one and he better hope he only has two.*

He continued the sweetness through the night and then I told him I had to leave. He offered to take me home. I said no, but that I would have his driver take me.

"Hmm, you are one tough cookie, but I'm in this baby. Why don't you allow me to take you to dinner this weekend?"

"I'll let your driver know and give him instructions." Wow, I felt like one powerful mofo, like *Devil Wears Prada*. I liked it.

On the weekend his driver picked me up and I met him at an upscale place. He was sitting waiting for me and I was still feeling the power. After we got our drinks, he said, "I don't like dating girls. I love real women who know who they are and what they want out of life."

"Well, that's a bold statement, but somewhat rehearsed.

Give me something more original," I said. *Wow, I'm giving this guy the gears!*

Throughout dinner, fans and people wanting photo ops kept interrupting us and he seemed to be eating it up. Meanwhile, *I* was eating up my delicious dinner. When the manager came over and asked if we would like to be moved to a private booth he said no. So what came out of his mouth next was, well, things that make you go "hmmm".

"Look, I'm an old soul and I value real connection and understanding. I've just never been much for all of the hype that comes with success and fame," he said, his Stanley Cup ring glistening almost as much as his diamond encrusted watch.

"Oh, tell me more," I said sarcastically.

"You don't believe me do you?" he asked.

"Not really. Listen, I have no issues whatsoever with anyone's success and fame, but when someone is speaking one thing and living another, I call BS." I was no longer feeling the rush of power. I was just feeling over it. "Look, I'm sure you're a nice enough guy and we have had some interesting conversations, but this isn't going to go anywhere."

"See, that's what I mean, you *know* what you want and you won't settle for less. I really want to be a part of that."

He was a persistent bugger, wasn't he? I knew in my heart and ever-astute brain that this dude wasn't a good choice for me, bling and fame aside.

"I appreciate you acknowledging those qualities in me, but spending more time with you is really making it evident that we're not a match. It was nice to meet you," I said as I put my napkin on the table.

"That's it huh? Would it change your mind if I gave you box tickets to my next game?"

"Nope. See you around."

I would still see him around the city at events and he would always just stare at me creepily. He phoned a few times and, when I blocked his number, he kept calling me from different numbers. I just kept blocking those too.

Penalty for interference dude, but you ain't getting into *this* box.

JOHN #20

So, back to the older men now. John #20 was about 10 years older than me, a retired pilot, had just finished building his dream home on the island, and seemed to be a pretty chill guy. He had a very mature way about him, but also had intelligent humour that was refreshing. We met in the afternoon for a walk and talk and had said that we would play it by ear if we carried on for dinner.

He was lighthearted, a real gentleman, and was stimulating my mind with his conversation. He was kind of like a professor type—interesting to listen to, but a little stale in the "va-va-voom" category. Now, the thing was, since he didn't live here, he was staying out by the airport because he took the puddle jumper over. So if we were going to continue on to dinner, he suggested that we should go out there. He said that he would either pay for my taxi back into town or my own hotel room and that he would be the perfect gentleman. *Hmm, why the heck not?*

We went for dinner and were getting along pretty good, but still no fireworks. On paper and in person he was acceptable, but... I needed extraordinary. Thinking that maybe more conversation (and by conversation, I meant more wine) might make him more appealing, we went for a nightcap in the bar. Still nothing. So, I called it a night and we went to our respective rooms. No kiss, just a friendly side hug. I locked, steel barred, and chained my door. Can't be too careful you know.

As I started washing my face, I heard a knock on the door and went to look through the peephole. It was John #20, surprise, surprise. He was standing there in the hallway in his bathrobe with a bottle of wine and two glasses. *Shit. Do I ignore him or tell him to go away?*

"I see you at the peephole Jill," he said in a weird sing-songy voice.

"Go away. I'm getting ready for bed and I'm not interested in having you come in."

Silence. I looked out again and saw him walking away.

Okay, that was easy.

The evening was pretty uneventful, with no more unwanted knocking at my door, but my phone was another thing. When I woke up and wiped the sleep from my eyes, I looked at my phone to see that I had missed 10 calls and six texts from John #20. *Sigh. Why can't this be easy?* I had figured that I would eventually just meet him down in the lobby and say, "Thank you, but we're not a match." But, then a knock on my door made me think otherwise.

I went to look through the peephole and there he was, in his bathrobe *again! Not good. So much for him being the perfect gentleman.* I walked back to the couch and phoned him.

Yeah, I was a little flustered and I didn't want to communicate through the door.

"Look, we had an agreement that we wouldn't even go there. This is making me really uncomfortable," I implored.

"Well, I'm really attracted to you, but I can see now that the feeling's not mutual," he said.

Well, duh. "I'm not interested in you romantically. Things don't always work out as you want them to, but we gave it a shot," I said sympathetically.

"Okay then, do you want me to get you a taxi to drive you home?"

"No, I will. Thanks John #20. It was nice to have met you and I wish you well in your search for the right woman for you."

What? A little too trite? Pfffft.

Now for the head spinning part.

After I surmised the coast was clear, I left the hotel. My phone had long since died from all of the unwanted activity, so I was unaware of the lengthy email that was being crafted by crazy-pilot-man. When I got home I plugged my phone in and went to my computer and was greeted with no less than five emails.

"Take heed of your soul, listen to your spirit and continue to be a spiritual person, but that might not be enough because you must be warned of the wolves that surround you."

What the hell? Was he talking about himself? Did he think that he was a wolf? He went on and on about the end of the world and being prepared and it was cuckoo I tell you! Cuckoo! I deleted all of his messages and then I got a text (damn phone had been recharging and I hadn't blocked him yet).

"So, did you get home safe and sound? I really care about you and hope that all is well." BLOCK. BLOCK. BLOCK. For the love of god, CALL BLOCK!

And then I called a priest, just in case I needed some exorcism action.

JOHN #21

H E WAS A DOCTOR!!! (I know John #10 was too, but he was just yucky!) Did that mean he'd be normal? Okay, not *too* normal. He needed to have a little excitement about him, just not have multiple personalities or weird sexual fantasies. He was also a runner, a wine lover, and he lived in a very prestigious area. We had a couple of great conversations before we agreed to meet at a gorgeous restaurant that he had suggested close to his neighbourhood. Yes, I really was branching out and expanding my horizons.

He was a little shorter than I would have liked, but his taste in wine was exquisite and his stories of travel were fascinating. He had been to Africa, France, Transylvania (not sure about that one) and the Swiss Alps. He even told me a very touching story about a family that he had met in a village on an excursion in Africa and how friendly and giving they were. He said that they stopped again at the village on the way back and found out that the little girl had died from drowning when she was washing her family's clothes in a river. Both of us were crying buckets of tears at the table and seemed to find a bond with that sad story.

He told me more about his practice and said that he was a specialist. He also spoke at some medical conferences that were fun to go to because he met colleagues from all around the world. Plus, our food was glorious! He had a massive rack of lamb and I had the osso buco and we basked in our meat sweats together. It was awesome! At the end of the night, I asked him where he parked and he said he didn't bring his car so asked if I could drive him home. He said he lived only five minutes away. *Umm, okay. I've never driven a date home before, so this will be a first.* On the bright side, I'll get to see his house and plan the renovations for when I become a doctor's wife!

His house was decent and very similar to my last house. *Hmm, I really thought this was going to be an upgrade.* We hugged awkwardly in the car ('cause, unless you're naked with your feet up against the windshield, it's always just awkward) and agreed that we would go on another date.

He decided that he would like to take me to dinner and a movie (I'm not really a big movie buff, with all of those people in such close quarters and someone always kicking your chair) and we'd meet at the new Italian place a block away from the theatres.

As you know, I had been dating A LOT and it was hard to keep track. Texting friends on top of it all was challenging, trying to keep everything straight. I had told a girlfriend that I had met a doctor and she was pretty stoked, so we were back and forth with conversation.

"I wonder if the good doctor's gonna make a move on me

in the dark movie theatre? Hubba Hubba." *Send. Nooo! Shit. Shit. Shit.* I didn't send it to my girlfriend, I SENT IT TO THE GOOD DOCTOR!!!

I waited, nothing. I messaged my girlfriend and let her know what had just happened. She told me she had just peed herself. You gotta admit, it *was* pretty funny. Still nothing from the doctor, though. *Oh well.* I figured if he didn't have a good sense of humour with this, then we weren't compatible anyways. Finally he texted back.

"So see you at 6:00 then?" That was it.

Weird. I wonder if he's playing the straight man role, you know when all of the sudden they come out with a zinger? Nope, still nothing.

I replied, "Sounds good," and we met at the restaurant.

I felt like asking him about the text and having some fun with it, but all of the sudden he was way more serious than before. So, we sat. He said he couldn't have a glass of wine because he'd be driving (in four hours!) and proceeded to order a blue cheese and capicola pizza with half the meat. *Okay, where did the guy from the other night go?* Our conversation wasn't flowing like it had been before, so I thought it must be about the text. Since I'm not one to leave things hanging, I finally said, "Hey, did you get that funny text that I sent earlier?"

He just looked at me.

"You know, the one where I said, "I wonder if the good doctor..."

"Oh that! Yes I did."

"Aaaand?" I cocked my head sideways in confusion.

He took another bite of his pizza.

"Did you think it was funny at all?" I asked.

"Yes! I thought it was quite humorous. I even shared it with my assistant and she thought so too." *So, I see that communication is not his strong suit.*

It was finally time to go to the movie. He had about a quarter of his pizza left and he wanted to take it to the movie with us. *Really?* It was pretty stinky and greasy, but hey, if the doc wanted his pizza to go, then gosh darn it, he was gonna take it to go.

We got to the theatre and it was already packed, so we had to squeeze into the middle of a row (which I abhor!). I tried not to touch anything, but you know how hard *that* is. He got us both waters and a small popcorn to share and he still had his smelly pizza that was starting to permeate a 10 foot parameter. I could even hear comments from people a couple rows down: "What's that smell? Bad sweatsocks or something?"

I shrunk in my seat, thinking that would help.

The movie started and it turned out to be a very dark movie about murder and depressing people and just blah. *Great choice doc.* We remained in our respective cones of silence and there was no touching, which by this time I was sooo okay with. It was clear that John #21 was not going to make it to date three. There were too many odd things about him that would drive me bonkers.

The movie ended and I said thanks and that I was just going

to go home now. He asked me *again* if he could have a ride, but this time to his car and he *still* had his fermented pizza! We walked to my car and he asked if I would please just drop him off at the hospital because that's where his car was. I guess he had never heard of a taxi service before. I pulled up in front of the hospital and was trying to be all positive,

"Thank you so much for the nice dinner and my wine was delicious!"

"Oh, I liked the company the best myself," he replied.

"Oh, um, yeah, thanks," I said awkwardly as I patted him on the shoulder like he was diseased.

Doctor, there will be no house calls.

JOHN #22

"Jill, you HAVE to come to this anniversary bash at this high-end jewelry store tonight! You MUST!" my friend begged.

"Why, Sugar?" I asked, intrigued.

"I just met this guy and he is *so* your type. He's tall, successful, funny, generous, smart…shall I go on?"

"No, sounds good, but what about his face? You know I'm not shallow, but I want to be prepared and keep my expressions out of the 'ewww zone'."

"He's nice looking, a little older, but in really good shape and he dresses pretty well. But, that can always be upgraded, you fashionista, you!"

I came into the spectacular jewelry store and, aside from all of the beautiful sparkly things, it was hard to pick what amazed me more—all of the plastic faces that looked identical (same plastic surgeon?), or how they could balance on those tiny stilettos with their enormous bobbly-boobs sticking out of their pricey couture. I saw my friend and she grabbed me a glass of champagne as she came over to hug me. "Darling, I am so glad that you came. It's all the who's who and it wouldn't be the same without you here!" she squealed.

"Thanks for having me sweetie. So where's Mr. Right?" I asked, not wasting any time.

"Oh, see all of those gold diggers?"

"Which ones?" I said with a laugh.

"Funny girl! He's right over there in front of the engagement rings. Oooo, how perfect! Maybe it's a sign. Now, go get him guuurl!" she said.

I wandered over and tried to eavesdrop on his conversation, but was a little too obvious.

"So, what's a nice girl like you doing eavesdropping on a guy like me? Haha!"

"Darn, you caught me!" I said with a laugh.

"I'm John #22 and you must be Jill. Your friend told me all about you. I've been keeping my eye on the door for you and saw you talking to her, so I guessed that was you. How are you doing?"

"Oh pretty good thanks. This is a gorgeous store isn't it? I love the old architecture that they've restored," I said.

"Your friend said that you were cut from a different cloth and not like the *rest* of the crowd here and she was right. Here we are in one of the most opulent jewelry stores and you are just loving the old artistry of the building. I'm intrigued to get to know you more."

He was pretty intense the way he was completely focused on me even with all of the baubles and boobies around.

"Well, that's me, Lil' Miss architecture."

Even though he was older than I wanted, (again with these older guys who are drawn to my energy and zest for life and then need to take naps) we talked until the champagne stopped. It was time *this* Cinderella went home. He asked if he could take me out the next evening and I said yes.

We met at fabulous resto with a new chef who everyone was raving about. His intensity didn't let up. He continued to be a really close talker and was fully captivated by everything I had to say. The closer he came though, the more I could smell something that wasn't very pleasant. I wasn't sure if it was something he had stepped in or maybe had spilled on himself. I just couldn't quite place it. Anyways, we were getting quite a few stares from the other tables, mostly older businessmen wondering what gramps was doing with me, I suppose. We talked a lot about childhood memories of cereal (strange, but true) and business and he was very interested in my opinion regarding marketing and such. It was a good conversation, but I was more bent on "How can I make some money off this guy and get a consultation fee?"

We went to a wine bar afterwards where it was a little quieter and talked more about his business. Then out of the blue he shared with me, "I'm not able to pee by myself."

I choked on my wine.

"It's a problem with being flaccid. I have to stick a tube into my penis. I have it right here," he said, as he pulled it out of his pocket.

I choked again. *Ewwww.* Now, it dawned on me; *That's what I could smell on him—pee!* My face contorted and I pushed back in my seat.

"Oh, don't worry, I always wash it before I put it back in my pocket," he said.

My mind was racing with all sorts of things, like most importantly can he get it up sexually? Not that I was interested in having sex with him, but now I was just curious.

"Sooo, what about, you know, being intimate and all that?" I asked.

"Oh, it works okay, but I must say, I prefer to please my partner orally."

That means it doesn't work.

Hmmm, now what to say?

"Hey, I'm really interested in helping you with your business. I would love to put together a proposal for some consulting. How does that sound?" I said in my executive voice.

"Sure, that would be great! Does that mean that you're not interested in dating me?"

"Well, you're a really nice guy, but I just don't see a romantic spark. I do see a connection to help you with your business though!" I said enthusiastically.

We met two days later. He signed off on the proposal, wrote me a cheque, AND gave me a box of Fruitloops. Good memory for a flaccid old fart.

John #23

What can 140 characters get you? Well, a date, in some cases. We had started to banter on Twitter and it was fun, but I banter with anyone who's got the *cojones*. We went back and forth about wine, real estate, social media—all things that were interesting to me. We agreed to meet. Now this was weird, because I didn't really know if it was a date or not. Were we meeting to talk about marketing, life, wine? Maybe I could get another contract with *this* guy!

We met in front of a resto on the water and it was packed. He said that he had put his name in, but we wouldn't get a patio table because it was too busy and the inside would be a while too. I just happened to know the GM, imagine that, so I went up to the front asked if he was kicking around. Sure enough, he was. He came over, took me in a full hug and swing, set me down, and promptly walked us to a table on the patio. Service with a swing and a smile? How do you like them apples?

This guy was super fun and he was catching the eyes of quite a few of the servers (from both teams). He seemed to take it all in stride. He was very interested in me and my adventures, so the conversation was flowing with laughter and hilarity. I still wasn't sure if it was a date or not.

As we talked, I kinda threw in some questions about previous dates and such. He seemed to be a real gentleman and never said a bad word about any of his exes. That was a good sign, unless of course he still went on holidays with them, like a couple of the previous Johns. That would be problematic. At the end of the date-ish, he asked if he could walk me home. I said, "Sure." I felt safe with this guy. Heck, I even knew his Twitter handle. If he tried anything bad, I would destroy him online. *Muah, ha, ha, ha, ha.* See, here's the thing. Unbeknownst to anyone at this point, I had an anonymous Twitter account where I would share EVERYTHING about my dates. No one knew who I was online, so it was a release of hilarity, astonishment, bewilderment and, in some cases, utter distain. It was brilliant. Anyways, back to John #23.

Yes, this was indeed a date, I surmised as he leaned in for one hot and steamy kiss when we were in front of my place. *Oooo.* I was tingling everywhere. We decided that date number two was a must. He would call me the next day and we would plan.

Three course dinner at his place with wine pairing? *Oh dear lawd, yes please.* It is so sexy when a man knows how to cook, how to pair wines, *and* how to release my innermost desires.

I got to his place and it was quaint with some very cool artwork and a pretty cool vibe. He was quite the gentleman, greeting me with a flute of champagne and chilled grapes (only thing was, grapes make me really bloated and gassy, unless, of course, they are the fermented kind). We sat on the couch and he started telling me about his travels and it was fascinating. I love to travel and hear about others' adventures. The conversation was going so well and then he leaned in and kissed me. The world stopped for a brief moment. He pulled back and looked into my eyes. I was in a daze, completely caught up in the sensuality of the moment, or maybe he put a roofie in my drink because I was feeling *fine* (*disclaimer: there was no roofie involved). He loved real estate, had a few new businesses on the go, and he was just damn exciting! He suggested that he start dinner and grabbed my hand to bring me up to the kitchen island so I could stare at his ass while he prepared dinner. Or was it so I could visit with him? *Hmmm.* Either way, he had one fine and very athletic ass, and was also very talented in the kitchen. After he served the first course and the wine was flowing, I found myself wandering into the kitchen wanting a taste of his lips. He gladly obliged. It was one hot kitchen.

We found ourselves on the couch after dinner in each other's arms, teasing each other with our lips, our touch. Scene close, but not in the "all in" sort of way, just enough that I need to protect your virginal eyes.

The evening was so much fun and it flowed so seamlessly, so when he called me the next day and asked if I would accompany him on his boat for a day on the water I said, "Hell yeah!" We went on a Saturday and it was ridiculously fun! Everything he did was just vibing (yes, I said it again) with me. We even talked about the possibility of taking a trip to Greece where he had a place. *I love Saganaki!* We sailed, kissed, fondled, sipped wine, it was heaven.

At the end of the date he asked if I would like to come over and I told him that I was going on a two day road trip the next day and leaving early in the morning, so I had to decline. I sooo wanted to be with him—in his arms, having him consume me—but responsibility took over. I was the one driving the next day, so I had to be sharp.

He messaged me early the next morning to wish me well on my short trip. He also said that he was going to go to some friends' place for a BBQ and that he wished I were there. *Awww, so sweet!*

Fast forward two more days. He had messaged while I was away, but not with the sensual fervor that he had previously, so my spidey senses were up. I called him on it when he phoned me.

"Hey, what's up with you?" I asked.

"Oh Jill, this is so hard. I didn't mean for it to happen."

Here we go... "What happened John #23? I'm a big girl. Lay it on me," I said.

"Well, at that party I went to the day you went away, my old girlfriend was there and we kinda hooked up," he said sheepishly.

"Listen, you don't owe me anything. We're not in a relationship and if you're drawn back to your ex and you like recycling, then by all means go for it."

"But, I really like you and I want to see where this goes, and the confusing thing is, I still have feelings for my ex too."

Now *I* really wasn't feeling it. It's not that he did anything wrong, but I'm not a side dish to be served if it suited someone.

"Look, you're a really fun guy, but this isn't going to work. I wish you well pursuing your ex and hope that works out for you."

"I feel so bad. I feel like I ruined something that could have been so great and you don't even want to give us a chance."

"Well, you put your *chance* into someone else's vagina and I'm not into double dipping," I said, quite proud of my quick wit. "See you around John #23."

"But..."

Listen, finish what's on your plate first. If you leave it there and hunt for something tastier and then go back to it later, it'll be rotten. Hasn't anyone told you that salmonella's not good for you?

John #24

Now, I'm calling him John #24 like he was a legitimate date and went through the "process" when he didn't, but the memory of this story is just too fun not to share.

It all started off with tickets to the box for a big soccer game. I had invited a gaggle of girls and gays and the booze was flowing. Who was playing and what the scoreboard said was irrelevant. Who was getting a makeover and who was getting a shoulder massage was more in our wheelhouse. The evening was a blast and a girlfriend and I decided to carry it on afterwards at one of the hotspots in the city. We got there and it was like a reunion of sorts. People were calling my name, buying me drinks and just having a fun time. Who wouldn't like that?

All of a sudden, a bottle of champagne was presented to my girlfriend and me. Well, things were just getting better. I asked the bartender who the lovely individual was who was trying to ply us with expensive bubbles. He pointed over to a small man with a Cheshire cat grin on his face. *Well shit, this is gonna be fun.* The lil' fella came sauntering over and introduced himself.

"Hi, my name's John #24 and I'm celebrating a big merger

with one of my companies and wanted to share the moment with you. How are you lovely ladies doing?"

"Just fine thank you," I took the lead. "That's pretty exciting. Where's your team?"

"They were here celebrating earlier but it's just me left now."

Hmmm, dude is lonely and loaded. "Would you like some champagne?" I asked a little cheekily. After all, it *was* him who bought it.

"No, I'm good. I'm more of a scotch man anyways," he replied.

The night went on and we were thinking of calling it, so we said thanks to our champagne supplier and he said, "Why don't we take a tour of Vancouver in my limo and see the beautiful night?" Knowing that I could put him out with one poke to the head if I needed to (you know, the whole "stranger danger" thing), and also knowing that I really wanted to continue being spoiled, I said, "Sure!"

We piled into his limo and I gave directions to the driver to take us through Stanley Park as I opened a bottle of wine. We were singing and seat dancing. When we got to the middle of the park, I asked the driver to stop and my girlfriend and I got out and took some selfies with the beautiful bridge and the sparkly stars in the background. It was pretty magical until... "Hey, would you like to dance in the moonlight?" John #24 asked.

Oh, I kinda forgot about him. "No, I'm good thanks. I'm hungry!" I said, as we got back in the limo.

"Where would you like to eat? It's almost 2:00 am, so I'm not sure what's open," he said.

"Gyro! I know a great place!" I said as I gave the driver directions to where I could fill my belly. *Food awaits!*

We ordered a table full of food and clearly my eyes were bigger than my belly because I just hit a wall.

"I'm sleepy," I said, starting to feel like another one of the seven dwarfs. "We have to go. Thanks for everything!" I said as we got up to leave.

"But, wait. What about me? I kinda thought that the three of us could go back to my place and have a night cap."

"No, you said that you wanted us to celebrate with you and we did. G'night."

Guys, if you want to buy a lady a drink, buy her one. No expectations. If you want to take her on a limo ride, do it. No expectations. If you want to buy her a Gyro, buy her one. This time though, you can expect to take...the doggie bag home.

John #25

I had seen this guy around for a couple years at industry events and he exuded sexuality, but I was in a relationship at the time so never pursued anything. One night, at a wine tasting, he was standing at one of the tables and me and my wine courage went up to him and said, "Hey, I know you! You're, oh don't tell me, your name is Mark."

"Nope."

"Ummm, Jason?"

"Nice try. Good first letter though," he said as he smiled slyly at me.

"John #25!"

"Hey, you finally got it right!"

"I never forget a face," I said as I saddled up to the table beside him to get a taste...of the wine. We flirted and he talked about the wines that he liked and shared some of his canapes with me. Then my friends came up and were all in my face.

"Hey, so where do you want to go next?"

"I'm still hungry."

"I want to go to that new place."

When I turned around, John #25 was gone. Vanished. Disappeared. Vamoosed. Would that be the last I saw of John

#25? *Dunn, dunn, dunnnnnn.* Apparently not because this chapter's about him.

About two weeks later, I was at a party of an acquaintance and it was going pretty well. I was talking to some fun people and eating some delicious food when all of the sudden John #25 came in, walked straight towards me and consumed my lips in his. Holy hell, it was hot! He stepped back and asked, "Do you remember my name?" with a wink.

"It's Mark, don't be silly!"

"Hey, I didn't mean to just leave without saying goodbye the other night at the wine tasting, but you looked like you had your hands full. What did you get up to?" he asked.

"Oh, we just went out for a bite and ran into some more friends, so had drinks with them. You?" I asked.

"I just went home had some cuddles with my dog."

Okay, he needs to stop that right now because it's making me all mushy inside.

We laughed and talked some more and then we walked out onto the deserted patio and had a pretty serious kissing session. I was becoming quite the kissing bandit. We kissed into the wee hours of the morning, with some minor interruptions from people coming out for a smoke, and then he asked if he could drive me home. Okay, I was breaking the rules again, but I figured we had a lot of people in common, so a drive home would be okay.

He pulled up front and we kissed a little more and he asked

if he could call me. *Sure Lips Mckenzie. Let's see where this smoldering session will go from here.*

I had a friend's coming out anniversary party to go to and thought it inappropriate to bring my kissing buddy, so we agreed that he would meet me outside the gay bar at a certain time. It was a fun little get together; we even had a cute little musical artist named Carly Rae "Call Me Maybe" come to celebrate with us. I had told my friend about the guy I was meeting and he was giddier than a schoolgirl, he was so excited. He kept on looking out the window to see if my date had showed up and when he was outside my friend squealed, "Oh my gawd! He is absolutely smoldering! Go to him guuurl!"

"He can wait a little minute. It'll make him want me more," I replied with a smile. There was something about this situation that I felt completely in charge of.

When I finally stepped outside and we hugged, I couldn't help but giggle as I looked in the window to see my friends' face pasted against it to get a closer look. Then John #25 took me to this quaint little French bistro. Unfortunately, we had a cramped seat in the corner with Nosy Nellies at our elbows. We started talking and I found him to be a little too inquisitive, especially in such a tight space. He was asking way too many private questions, or maybe I just didn't want to answer them. Either way, I wasn't interested in this serious stuff. I just wanted to get it on. *Dear god, I'm becoming a male.* With anyone else it was always about the waiting game, but somehow this was different. I wasn't interested in getting to know him anymore. I was just interested in what he could do for me, or better yet, *to* me. *Well, I'm a consenting adult. Let's get it on.*

We got back to my place and started to mess around. It was hot, it was raw and it was emotionless (for me, at least).

"Okay, thanks for coming over," I said as I went to get some water.

"What? You mean that's it?" he said in disbelief.

"Yup. See, what we have here is an arrangement. What happens here doesn't leave this place," I said as I made circles with my hands. "If I ever see you in public, we can acknowledge that we know each other, but beyond that, there's nothing."

"Seriously?" he was still in shock.

"Yup. I guess if you need to label it, it's called a Pillow Pal. If you're not up to it then..."

"No, it's just that...well, no one has ever been like this with me before. It's gonna take some getting used to," he said.

"Listen, I don't want anything serious right now," I said, which was the truth. I just needed to have a safe, reliable Pillow Pal for that moment in time and John #25 fit the bill.

No shame here people. This stuff happens ALL the time. Your friends are just too prude to tell you about it. Just like a mouthwatering steak after you've been on a silly juice cleanse, it satisfies your carnal need. 'Nuff said.

John #26

So after my Pillow Pal phase with John #25 was finished, I slowly got on the man wagon again. And by slowly, I mean I jumped right into the deep end again. John #26 was an older guy, again with the love of fine wine and good food. He had spent 10 years in Italy and that, to me, along with everything else, was a clincher for a date. We met at one of my neighbourhood pub-ish type places that I had never been to and then I found out why. I was the only one there without a man bun. I couldn't see my date when I came in, so I took up a perch in the front corner where I could be amused and entertained by my subjects. As I ordered my wine, I noticed a rather nervous looking older man who was quite nice looking, but who seemed to have some kind of tick or something. He came right towards me, said hello, and told me that I was even more ravishing in real life. *Well, have a seat kind sir! You are my date, right?*

He talked about his travels to Europe and his time in Italy. His son, who apparently was now in France training to be a chef, had spent his formative years in Italy and fell in love with food. *Hmm.* As I was looking at him, I was thinking that his son was probably closer to my age than he was. Every once in a while he would do a little head bob side to side. I wasn't sure what was causing it, but I didn't want to be rude and ask him. He *seemed* like he was a lovely man and I wasn't sure if he could be romantic material, but the conversation was still lively and enjoyable. He asked if I was hungry and I said I was a little. We both mulled over the menu and realized that people with man buns have weird taste in food. He asked if I would like to go to another spot that was a well-known Indian place just around the corner. "Sure, let's do it," I replied. So we walked over. Something about being closer to him though gave me a *déjà vu* about his scent. *What was it?* It was kinda off, but I just couldn't place it.

We got a seat and his head-shaking was a little more pronounced than before. The server came over and asked if we wanted something to drink, but it was right when his head was moving and she thought he was shaking his head "no", so she walked away. He was getting irritated and I was at a bit of a loss as to what to do. Finally he said, "I had a stroke and when I get nervous my neck moves involuntarily and people think that I'm shaking my head at them."

"Oh, I'm sorry. Why don't we just call her back and start again?" I said as I motioned her over. "Look, I wasn't shaking my head. I've had a stroke and we would appreciate some service," he blurted out.

Hmm. I understand that he's frustrated, but this young thing had no clue and he really should be nicer.

"Um, okay," she replied.

He ordered some wine and seemed to withdraw into himself.

We carried on and ordered some tasty bits, but the conversation never really took off again. In fact, he got more ornery and was clearly off-put by his physical difference being brought out in the open. I can understand it would be hard to accept initially, but don't you think that the sooner you accept it and embrace it the better off you are? Anyways, I'm not one to preach. It makes no difference to me. I just want someone who is positive and embraces life, and either works with what life brings them or changes it.

Now, here's the bizarre thing. He excused himself to use the restroom and I saw that he pulled out a tube JUST LIKE JOHN #22 HAD! So *that* was that familiar smell: pee! How the hell did I score two guys that had the same issue?

He came back to the table and I was more than finished with this date. I politely said, "Thank you for the nice time."

He said, "It's that damn stroke isn't it?" in an angry voice.

"No, it's your damn attitude," I said.

"Well, if it wasn't for the stroke I wouldn't have to be so angry," he said.

Whoa. This wasn't something that I wanted to get into.

I have no issue with someone's physical ailment. What I do have an issue with is someone blaming the world for his or her own shitty attitude. Dollars to donuts this guy was a bitter old man before the stroke.

Mmm, donuts.

John #27

A dentist! *Nice. Free teeth whitening if all goes well?* He was a cowboy on his ranch by the ocean when he wasn't drilling teeth. I was a little apprehensive about the cowboy part, but the ocean sho' nuff got my attention (see what I did there?).

We met at a new Mexican tapas place that everyone was raving about. It was right at the intersection that I called 12th and Lesbian (just for some background, people). We got there at the same time and the place was packed. I saw two seats at the bar and we agreed that we would sit there instead of waiting for a table.

As we were getting somewhat comfortable with each other, I was looking around the room. *Hmm, there's a lot of lady couples, as in, there aren't any men.* Seriously, as I was looking around, we were the only hetero people in there. There were a lot of half-shaved heads with Krishna ponytails and one lady sitting with her two kids had a tattoo on her forehead. Yes, a tattoo right in the middle of her forehead that trailed off into her hair like a Charles Manson groupie. It was spooky.

I got back to looking at the menu and then I *really* started to panic. I could deal with tattoo head, but this? *No, it can't be true.* There was no meat on the menu. *Noooooo!* My eyes got wide as I flipped the menu over. *Nothing but vegetables! Why was everyone raving about it? What was so...oh.* I saw on the back that they were mentioned as a place for breakfast. *What the hell? You might not serve bacon, but you serve eggs and eggs are meat you veggie-heads! Don't be fooled. They grow up to be chickens.*

"So, what's looking good to you?" John #27 asked.

I had almost forgotten about him, I was in such a state. "Umm, I'm really not a vegetable person. I was looking forward to a piece of meat," I said.

"Oh reeeeeally?" he said with a laugh. "And what kind of meat would *that* be?"

"What?" Oh, I could see that he was trying to be funny, but this was no laughing matter. I was a meat girl, damn it, and I wouldn't be fooled into eating at a vegetarian place. They didn't even have it on their sign outside! *How dare they?*

We ended up leaving and going to a chain restaurant because by now I could have eaten a horse and I needed some meat in my belly STAT! After the meatless scare, I was able to calm my nerves down a bit and ask him some more questions about his life. Turned out he was quite odd; he kept on second-guessing things I would say. That drew me to the conclusion that he was also very insecure and that is a real turn off, *am I right ladies?* I had an out though because I had told him earlier that I had a charity event I had promised to pop in at that evening. Would I like a drive there in his Porsche, he asked. *Nah, Porsche's aren't meant for cowboys. Only ladies should be drivin' those toys. You might be able to rustle up some fillies back at the other restaurant though. They might even take you for a ride...a looong ride. 12th and Lesbian, no meat allowed. He-he-he.*

JOHN #28

He lived in the burbs, but spent most of his time in the city because of his construction company and his hockey team. I know what you're thinking; wasn't the *other* hockey player warning enough? John #28 played in a men's league to stay in shape, so that was reasonable.

We met at a private tennis club that he belonged to (okay, we *all* know that was one of the reasons I agreed to go on a date with him) in the restaurant. It was one of those clubs where it was mostly old money with spoiled trust fund babies. I wasn't sure which category he fell into yet. Our conversation was fun—a lot of jokes, mostly coming out of my mouth. But, I wasn't *completely* steamrolling him. *Yay team Jill.*

We got past the drinks and he asked if I was hungry. *Cha! I'm always either hungry or sleepy, no in between.* I looked at the menu and when he asked what I was thinking, I said, "Oh, I think the prime rib. I love it and not many places serve it, or if they do, they don't serve it properly. Have you had it here?"

"Uh, no. I'm more of an appetizer kind of guy. I've seen it though and it's a pretty big serving. Are you sure you can handle it?" he said.

What? Is he my mother? "Listen Sugar, I've had a lot of meat in my mouth, and I think I can handle it," I replied. Now, if that wasn't a WIDE open opportunity for him to shoot me a zinger, I don't know what was. Nothing. *Is this guy becoming a dud or is he just still shy?*

The night went on and it did get better. He started getting more comfortable and making some funnies. So, we agreed to another date.

We planned to meet at a restaurant and then walk to a comedy club for a show. On the day of the date, I dressed down a little in my jeans because I had been the fodder of too many comedians' sets about being "Miss Fancy" and I really just wanted to be in the background that night.

As I walked into the restaurant, I got a text from him saying that traffic was brutal and he would be a few minutes late. *Fair enough.* We still had plenty of time before the show. I ordered some wine and settled in.

"Guuuurl! What are you doing here? It's been forever!" said one of my gays as he threw his arms around me.

"Oh, hey! What are *you* doing here?" I asked.

"Oh, since my Sugar Daddy left me high and dry, quite literally, I've had to get a job. Ewwww! I started working here a couple weeks ago," he said.

"Oh honey, I'm so sorry! You do know, though, that *most* people work for a living, don't you?" I said with a wink.

"Oh, I know. It's just so pedestrian though. Who are you meeting?" he asked.

"A date. We're going to the comedy club after. He's stuck in traffic right now."

"Well, you're not in my section, but you can bet your cute booties that I'll be keeping my eye out to see who this man is who is taking up your time," he said as he air kissed me and left with a twirl.

Out of the corner of my eye, as I was sipping my wine, I could see what looked like either Rocky Balboa or a street thug coming in with a hoodie on. *What the hell punk? We don't take your kind here*, was what I was thinking when the thug stopped at my table and sat down. It was John #28.

"Hey, sorry I'm a little late," he said as he pulled back his hood.

"What's with the hood, Rocky?" I couldn't resist.

"Oh, I was at the gym earlier and I always wear my hoodie after I hit the showers," he replied. "Indoors too, I see," I said.

"Well, I wasn't sure where you were sitting and I didn't want to look awkward when I came in." *Lame. Grow some balls buddy.* "Hmm, so are you going to order a bevy?" I asked.

"No, I'm not much of a drinker and the drink I had the other night was one of my twice yearly." *Oh boy.* Was this *another* one with issues? Just to check, I ordered another glass of wine and my glass wasn't even half empty yet. He didn't even flinch. *Okay, at least Rocky's okay with my wine consumption.* And to be clear, I wouldn't be the one to change if he *did* have an issue; it would be the door for him.

We ordered some food and keep chatting, nothing earth shattering or heart pulsing though. My friend kept trying to get my attention from across the restaurant and I kept ignoring him. This introduction would be too awkward. This dude was probably not gonna make date three at this rate.

John #28 said that he already bought the tickets for the comedy club and they were at will call. *Okay, things are looking up, just a bit.* We settled the bill (meaning, he paid) and we started walking the three blocks to the club.

"How'd you get in those jeans girl?" he sang in a Texan twang to me.

"Pardon?" I said as I stared at this strange thug of a cowboy.

He started laughing. He said that he was driving his sons to their hockey practice (Oh, I didn't mention he had sons, did I? Oh well, his story isn't that long so it didn't warrant it) and that song came on the radio.

"Oh, how, um, quaint," I replied. *Shit, I'm in for another weirdo, aren't I?*

We got to the club and he went to the will call and I heard the woman say, "You here for the mingler?"

"Yeah, yeah, thanks," he said as he got us scanned in.

"Mingler?" I asked.

"Oh, haha. It's nothing. We're just here for the show. I'll go get you some wine," he said as we got to our table.

He turned and went to the bar. *Something is definitely odd here.* I looked around and there was a LOT of estrogen in the room, which was unusual for a regular comedy night. A big area was all sectioned off, but I couldn't quite read what the table tents said with the lights so low.

Rocky came back with a carafe of wine for me and two beers for himself. *So much for him not drinking much.* He sat down, pretty much drained his first beer and said, "Sometimes you just need a cold one to quench your thirst." I just looked at him with my head cocked sideways. It wasn't adding up. *Oh good, the announcer is coming on stage. At least I can lose myself in this and laugh a little.*

"So, how many of you losers are here for the Matchmaking Mingler?" he teased at the sectioned off area.

Are you freakin' kidding me? He got tickets when he knew this was a matchmaking thing? I immediately asked him, "When did you get these tickets?"

"About a week before I met you and I didn't want them to go to waste so I thought…" he trailed off.

"You thought wrong you moronic waste of skin. So, you wanted to see what else was out there on the premise of taking *me* on a date? Holy hell buddy, this is a first."

"But, but…" he tried as I got up to leave.

"Hey Blondie, it's too early to leave, we haven't even started the first act yet," shouted the announcer.

Shit! Why am I always part of the show? "I was just making sure that my parolee wasn't around any minors. He has a 100-foot court-imposed rule. He's all yours now sport," I said as I pushed through the doors.

Who's the thug now, homie?

John #29

A girlfriend was nursing her broken heart on a Saturday night and asked me to come along to be a part of the mending, i.e. designated driver, drink watcher, and bodyguard. We were at a club that I hadn't been to in ages, so it was kinda fun to see some of the staff's familiar faces, albeit much older. My friend was lamenting about her life while I was ensuring that she didn't fall of her chair. A hockey game had just ended, which was the sole reason for her wanting to come to this place because it had started raining men. *Hallelujah!*

She was in and out of lucidity, but kept pleading that we stay. *Okay, take one for the team and all that.* So, we stayed. She danced a little with some vetted partners and with my eyes on her like a hawk to make sure she wasn't taken advantage of. Yup, I was full on mama-bear, all the way. She came back up to our table and sipped on the very tall soda water with lime that I had gotten her, which she thought was the biggest vodka EVER. I had just resigned myself to a night of continued babysitting when a beautiful piece of chocolatey goodness walked up the stairs. *Good heavens above.* This man was a god. We locked eyes for a moment.

"Jill, hey, is there any alcohol in this?" my dear friend asked.

"I'm not really tasting anything." "No sweetie. You're not tasting anything because you're already three sheets to the wind," I replied. I turned my head back to the stairs. *Shit.* My Adonis was gone. *Wait a minute.* There was a smallish guy standing there on the stairs with a shit-eating grin. *What the hell does he want?* He started walking over to our table with his smile still a mile wide.

"Hey, I saw you looking at me and I am so flattered because you're so beautiful. I'm John #29, so nice to meet you," he said with such innocence I didn't have the heart to tell him that I had been looking at a chocolate Adonis, not a movie extra.

He started talking and actually turned out to be a really sweet guy. He was also with some friends who were turning it up while he was on guard duty. He asked if he could sit for a while and I said sure. My friend had her head resting on her arms on the table anyways. Classy, I know. We talked for about half an hour and then I said that I really needed to get my friend home while she could still lean on me. He said that he understood and said goodbye.

I got my friend propped up and started maneuvering her through the crowds right when one of the old bouncers came over and asked if he could help. *God bless him.* We got to the front door and the little guy came running up the steps towards me all out of breath.

"Hey, I couldn't just leave without giving you my number, I would kick myself forever if I did that. I'm going to be out of town starting Monday for work. Then I'll be back and forth for the next couple months. I would love it if you called," he said.

"Oh, okay, thanks," was all I had in me at that moment.

A couple weeks went by and I was cleaning out my purse and there it was—his phone number. *Hmmm, what to do? Do I call? Nah? Should I?*

"Hey, it's Jill. We met at the bar a couple weeks ago. How are things?"

"Heyyy! I totally thought you threw away my number. It's so nice to hear from you," he replied in a voice that was far deeper and sexier than I remembered.

"So, where exactly are you?" I asked.

"I'm in Iowa. I'm here to start growing a business with a couple other people," he said.

"Oh, what kind of business?"

"It's kind of complicated. It's to do with farmers and working with them to make a protein substitute to sell to institutions."

Is he going to sell fake burgers to the mentally challenged because he thinks they won't know the difference?

"It's mostly for the prison population in the states. We've had studies done and there is a lot of money to be saved by them and made by us if we are able to change the way food is served there," he said.

"So is it a kind of tofu or something like that?" I asked.

"Yes, very similar. It's a brilliant product and it's very exciting to be on the breaking point of it," he said.

I was actually pretty excited for him too. If it meant big things for him, it meant sparkly things for me!

This phone thing went on for a couple weeks and it was wonderful. We didn't FaceTime, but we did send pics back and forth—tame ones for the most part. It was cool to speak with someone who was chasing his dream, for real. He was planning on coming back home for a few days and we were planning our date. It's odd when you feel so connected to someone, but you've only met once, yet have spoken to them on the phone every day for two weeks. *Will we kiss? Does he have good hygiene? Time will tell, I guess.*

He called me the minute he landed and said that he was so excited to finally see me again. I was excited too. We seemed to have so much in common on the phone and could talk for hours. It was interesting building a relationship on just conversation. I almost felt Amish—not that they talk on the phone, but that they don't really physically connect until, wait, do they ever connect before marriage? Anyways, we planned to meet at 7:00 pm for dinner at a pretty swanky place, so I put on my best "Welcome home, this is what you've been missing" outfit.

I arrived and the host ushered me to the table where John #29 was waiting for me. He stood up to greet me. He was A LOT shorter than I remembered and I wasn't even drinking the night we met. We went in for an awkward hug where he basically came up to my clavicle. *What the hell? Oh crap, I had my flats on the night I met him and never really stood beside him because he ended up sitting with me and my drunky-drunk friend. Great, and I opted for my 4 inch heels tonight completely forgetting that his height didn't match his voice.*

It's funny how conversations for two weeks can make you completely forget physical things. *Was it that important?* We *had* gotten along so well on the phone but this was—"Wow, you're a lot taller than I remember," he said.

"Yeah, and the heels kinda add another level," I said feeling like an Amazon.

The height thing seemed to be something that neither of us could get over. He asked if I always wore heels and I was tempted to ask if he ever wore lifts. Even if I *was* okay with shorty, he wasn't okay with me being "tally". We both knew that it wasn't going to work out and, after dinner, we gracefully said our goodbyes.

He was just going to have to sow his tofu oats somewhere else, like with the munchkins.

John #30

After our online pre-screening, we met up at a wine bar and the hilarity was flying. We were both on fire! He was a six-foot blond with blue eyes and had a little "Dennis the Menace" charm about him. He had a film production company (maybe I'd finally get my TV hosting gig) and loved to work out. He grew up in a small town and had small town values, but big city dreams. I was intrigued. Date number two was a must.

Date two was a Canucks vs Kings hockey game and he was a big fan of the Kings. In fact, he was such a fan that he always wore a Kings jersey and asked if I would too. *Sure, what the heck.* We met at a bar for a little tease before we walked to the arena. I put on the jersey and we were having a fabulous time. When we got in front of the arena, we took pictures with the mascot and anyone else who wanted to. We were just the dynamic duo.

Our seats were in the lower part right by the net, which was awesome. There were mostly Canucks fans in our area but all of them were good-natured and didn't threaten to burn our jerseys (or us). The game was fun; we kept meeting new people and it was like I was on a drug or something. Everything just seemed super awesome! *Let the good times role.*

After the game we decided we needed some more revelry and went to another bar close by. It was still a really fun time, but I was realizing it was becoming almost too "buddy buddy". I felt like I was one of the guys, shot gunning beer and scratching my balls, only not really. I needed a little more intel on this guy.

"Hey, when was your last relationship?" I asked.

"Oh, it ended about two years ago because she wanted to have sex and I wanted to save myself for marriage," he responded.

My eyes went wide. "Seriously? You're not pulling my leg are you?" I asked, knowing he was quite a joker.

"Nope, we were engaged to be married and went on a cruise with her family..."

"Wait, so you were engaged AND you went on a trip that consisted of overnights and nothing happened?"

"Well, we'd fool around, do some oral, but we had agreed to no actual sex."

"I hate to break it to you, but sex is sex," I said bewildered to be having this conversation with a grown man.

"I'm a Christian and I take my chastity very seriously," he said. "I don't think having 'oral' is sex and fooling around is okay, as long as there is no penetration."

Wow, this guy is something else. "Have you heard the term 'oral sex'? Well, it's *sex*, buddy. I can't believe that you are twisting it to fit into your own personal commandments. So, when your fiancé wanted to take the sex further, you said no and ended it?" I asked incredulously.

"Well, we actually did take it further on the last night and I felt so guilty that I broke up with her." *This guy is messed up.* "Well, you and I clearly don't have the same views, so this will end right here," I said.

"But why? We get along so well. I'll still mess around, but just won't do the deed," he said.

The deed? How old is this guy?

All I know is that my lady-bits need a *lot* more than a *little* bit of diddlin', otherwise I'd be in a nunnery. *Buh-bye.*

John #31

He wanted to meet at the park and walk his dog. Well, *that* was a new thing. I love four-legged dogs, so if it didn't work out, I would get my dog fix anyways. Actually, I don't discriminate; I'd love a three-legged dog too!

He was a lawyer who had two grown boys, was a partner in a law firm, and seemed to be "no nonsense" on the phone. I got to the park, sans high heels, and he looked like the older brother of the dude online. Upon closer examination, he looked like the older brother who was also heavier, had big boozy bags under his eyes, and a sloppy shirt. *Blech.* Again, fellas, don't lie; don't post a pic of your wonder years only to look in real life like you were ridden hard and put away wet.

He told me that his dog, Princess (and yes she was a fluffy little drop kicker), didn't like anyone, and for me not to be offended. *Buddy, I'm like the dog whisperer. All dogs love me.* Princess came over to give me a little sniff. I walked away from her and went to sit on a park bench. You have to be the pack leader with these pooches and show them who's calling the shots. So Princess came right over and sat at my feet. I gave her my hand to sniff a little more. Then I picked up the little pooch and we had a petting cuddle fest. John #31 was stunned. *C'mon, it's not that big of a deal. Dogs like me.*

"Wow, she honestly has *never* let a stranger get close to her. She's usually such a barky little thing," he said.

"Oh well, now she's not," I said as my little cuddle buddy enjoyed every moment.

John #31 sat down beside me and reached out his hand to pet his dog. She got up, went on the opposite side of me and cuddled right into me.

"Hey, why isn't she letting me pet her?"

"I don't know, she's pretty comfortable with the Pet Whisperer here. Just let her be for now," I said as I secretly schemed a way to dognap Princess.

We started talking more about our lives and he divulged that he had been married twice; the first wife was the mother of his two grown boys and the second wife was a demon from hell. *Oh my, doesn't that sound juicy!* Apparently, he had gone overseas on a "sexcation" and was in Thailand when he thought he found true love at the end of a fifty-dollar bill. She apparently was Canadian, but needed to make some money to get back home. He brought her back home to Canada with her four kids, married her, and then it all went to hell. This very "intelligent" lawyer had put all of his credit cards in her name too, opened up a bank account for her with a huge overdraft limit, bought her a brand new SUV, and got her all the plastic surgery she wanted. *Hey, if this putz was willing to pay for all of this when he only knew her for one week before he brought her home then, it's on him.*

She racked up all of the credit cards and her overdraft and then started going off on him physically all of the time, throwing things, ramming her SUV into his car—you know, all of the usual things couples in love do. He kept on putting up with it. Also, her kids were all teenagers and didn't have the best judgment (i.e. were spoiled, derelict punks). The oldest had a house-wrecking party, quite literally, that caused over $250,000 worth of damage. John #31 still wanted to keep this happy little family, so he just kept on letting it happen.

Here's where you should really shake your head. *She* left *him*! Yeah, she found another easy mark richer than this guy—who was equally as dull witted—and proceeded to shack up with him. After copious amounts of counseling and therapy John #31 saw that it wasn't a healthy relationship and now he was ready for real love.

Well, that's not going to happen with me, *buddy. I'm the dog whisperer, not the dude saver.*

JOHN #32

We met at an outdoor wine tasting and I initially thought he was a bit of a wanker. He pulled up in his Lambo and seemed kinda boyish but with an air of something I couldn't quite figure out. I did my best to ignore him at first, but he kept on following me and trying to a start a conversation. It turned out that a couple of my acquaintances knew him and they invited me to sit with them. *Okay, let's see what'cha got Richie Rich.*

He was telling me all about his global business, *yada, yada, yada.* Actually, he *was* Jewish; he came from money and wanted to make more. After a couple glasses of wine he didn't seem like such a loser. He was more genuine and started talking about more personal things. He said he was split from his wife, had two grown kids and was trying to make a difference in life. *Hmm.* These acquaintances seemed to vouch for him and kept on espousing his good qualities. The end of the night came. I had called my ride and John #32 came over and asked if he could drive me.

"No, I'm good thanks," I said.

"Well, I find you very intriguing and you clearly are a strong woman and I would love to get to know you better."

"Well, I'm not sure about you. You seem nice, but..." I trailed off.

"Wow, you don't even want to give me a chance? But I understand, you just met me. I really do wish you'd reconsider. I'll give you my phone number and leave it in your hands. I'm a good guy, honest Jill," he said as he wrote his number on a napkin and kissed my cheek.

Well, I tried to put him out of my mind, but there was some sort of boyish charm and worldly experience that kept goading me. Maybe it was his money... I left his number on my desk and carried on with my single-lady life. After almost two weeks, I thought, What the heck. I went to get his number and, with all of the coffee spills and condensation from my water bottle, I couldn't read two of the numbers. *Well shit.* Now that I was all ready to see what he was all about, my chance was gone. *Is love being elusive or is fate keeping me safe?*

I left it for another day and then thought, I *need* to try. I *had* to see if I could contact him. This was now a challenge that I had to conquer. With my number blocked, I started trying number combinations. I could only remember this guy's first name, so I couldn't even try directory assistance or Google. The first number was an old Chinese lady, the second number was out of service, and the third number—*hold on.* I got a voicemail and it was him! *Bingo!* I hadn't really expected to get anywhere with this exercise and hadn't thought of what to say on a voicemail. I blurted out, "Hey, it's Jill. I thought I'd give you that chance you asked for. Call me." Okay, that was short, sweet and bold. Good. Now we'll just wait and see.

That night he called back and he was so excited that I had reached out to him. It turned out that he was in Italy and it was first thing in the morning for him. He was over on a buying trip that he did quarterly, which immediately caught my "attenzione". Imagine shopping in Italy four times a year? My mind was racing with possibilities.

"Jill, are you still there?" he asked.

"Yes, of course. It must be the connection. So when are you back?" I asked.

"On the weekend. May I take you for dinner?"

"That would be lovely."

We talked for the next couple of days before he got back and the conversations were very interesting. It was so exciting and motivating to hear about someone's business, especially when they were across the world making it happen.

He wanted to pick me up at home, but I suggested that we meet for drinks first and then go for dinner so I could keep my three-date rule intact. He was dressed impeccably and I was of course in my finest flirty frock. He seemed very level and calm and very sweet. But don't they all...at first?

It was all good, so we agreed to carry on to dinner. We got outside and he had his Bentley this time. *Hmm, a different car for a different day of the week, buddy?* We got to one of my favourite restaurants and it was kinda funny because they knew us both and the treatment was over the top royalty. He knew the right foods and wine to order and it was cute because he did just that. Like an old-fashioned gentleman, he ordered everything for me and I felt like a princess—not to be confused with the Princess from the previous chapter. Woof.

It was magical—almost like Pretty Woman, but I haven't seen it yet, so I can only surmise. But, only in the generous rich man sort of way, not the prostitute part. He told me about his kids (who he was very proud of) and said that it was unfortunate, but it just didn't work with his ex. She was very bitter and superficial and was no longer the woman he fell in love with. That made sense. He sounded like he really wanted the finer things in life in the form of real love and connection.

The date ended and he asked if he could drive me home. Even though I felt safe and comfortable, I still said no, that I would get home from our pick-up spot.

Our next date was on his yacht. Yup, that's a big-ass boat. I was pretty excited as I packed my little bag with anything I thought I might need. Itty-bitty bikini, check. Sunscreen, check. Sexy dress for after, check. We met on the dock and he looked so handsome with his white linen shirt unbuttoned and his jeans partially rolled. I am a sucker for the Harlequin look. He was such a gentleman; he had everything that we could want for a day on the water. He had bubbly, wine, steaks, lobster, fruit and chocolate. *Damn, he might just get lucky on the high seas.*

It was beautifully serene on the water and I felt completely spoiled, like a woman should feel. He put the anchor down in a cove and we sipped bubbly while we shared stories. I was completely captured with his words. He had done so much, travelled to most parts of the globe and was starting new businesses—my kind of man.

My belly was telling me it was time to fill it and right on cue (maybe he heard it growling) he got up and started preparing our lunch. He did the steaks to perfection! And the lobster, don't get me started. He fed me lobster with butter dripping as we sat on the bow. Oh my gosh, I truly was floating in heaven on water. He just said all of the right things, did all of the right things and now I wanted to do all the right things to *him*. We started off with a long slow kiss that developed into more—much more.

Scene close.

I got home and I was on cloud nine. *How did I get so lucky?* This guy was showing to be a consummate gentleman, a talented businessman, a great conversationalist and potential lover. I was in la-la land as I drifted off for the night.

I woke up and turned my phone on to find three messages:

"You whore! How dare you have an affair with my husband."

"We have children. You probably don't understand the bond that a father has with their child and you're destroying it."

"It's all your fault that he doesn't find me attractive. How long has this been going on?"

Holy hell. I did not expect this. Just as I was finishing checking the messages, she called again. I let it go to voicemail, obvi. *Shit, this broad is on the warpath.*

I texted John #32 and asked him to call and said it was very urgent. My phone rang again and it was him this time.

"Hey bella, what's wrong? Are you okay?" he asked.

"Are you still with your wife?" I got right to the point.

"I told you I wasn't," he replied.

"I know what you *told* me. I'll ask you again, are you still with your wife?"

"Well, it's complicated," he tried.

"You bastard. Guess what I woke up to? Three, no make that four, irate messages from your wife. How the hell did she get my number?"

There was silence.

"Hello?"

"Babe, babe, look, I'm so sorry. She is one of the most insecure, jealous women I have ever known and she always goes through my phone."

"Aha! So you *are* still with her. That is beyond not cool John #32. Lose my number and I suggest you tell your wife to do the same. I'm done with you," I said as I hung up.

Now I was getting call after call from him *and* from her. Double block!

Moral: if you've got a crazy ass wife AND you're a cheater, don't try to bring *me* into the mix. Divorce her and move on, far away from me. I've never mud wrestled before and I ain't about to start now.

JOHN #33

John #33 was yet another entrepreneur who lived on one of the pricey sides of town and had a great sense of humour. We agreed to meet at a restaurant close to my place. I got there first and secured a booth at the back, which is kinda my thing, ordered some wine, and waited. I saw him come in, talk to the host, look around frantically and then walk back out. *That's weird. Didn't he see me? Should I text him? Nah, he's a grown man. Maybe he had to plug his meter or something.* A couple minutes later he came back in with the same frantic look on his face and scoped out the room again. He looked right at me and continued to look around more. *Um, hello?* He turned around my way again and this time he had put some glasses on. I gave a little wave and he took his glasses off as he came rushing over.

"Shit, I'm so sorry. Have you been here long?" he asked.

"Just long enough to see you come in the first time, leave and then come back in," I replied.

"It's an ego thing. I hate having to wear glasses, but I can't see squat without them."

"How many fingers am I holding up?" I said with a smile.

"Funny girl! I just need them for distance, so I always keep them in my car. Anyways, it's so wonderful to meet you. Are you hungry?"

"Honey, I'm *always* hungry!"

"Do you want to share some appies?" he asked.

"Sure! I love meat so anything protein related is good by me," I said.

"Oh, that's going to be a problem. I'm vegan."

Noooo, that's almost as bad as being married. "How long have you had this ailment?" I asked jokingly.

"It was a choice I made almost two years ago and it's done my body good. The only poison I put in is alcohol. After all, it's made from grains and fruit," he countered.

We joked and laughed and as I ate my meat I kept thinking, I could never be with a veggie head. It's just not in me. I love to share my food experiences and I love cooking a big meaty roast with all of the fixings. How would I deal with this blasphemy?

"Hey I heard about this new champagne lounge, do you want to go?"

Apparently, *that's* how you deal with it. "Okay!" I said, forgetting all about his meat shortcomings.

We taxied to the new swanky place and I was all giddy. *How have I not been here yet?* The decor was funky and the lights were low and the champagne was flowing. John #33 was in his element and was quite a jokester. He was zinging one-liners left and right and the tears were rolling out of my eyes. Right then he decided to give me a kiss and it landed smack on my teeth because I had been laughing so hard. He pulled back and, by the look on his face, I could see that the booze had finally hit him. Funny man was really drunk, and not the attractive kind. I guess we had been putting it back, but I had just as much as he did and I wasn't all sloppy. He got up to go use the washroom and was stumbling. *Not good.* I thought about bailing right there and then, but that would just be rude. I'd wait until he came back and then head out.

Tick, tick, tick. About 15 minutes later I thought, rude or not, I'm out of here. I got up to leave and, as I passed by the entrance to the washrooms, there he was passed out on the couch. *Classy.*

I got home and a text came through.

"Hey, where'd ya go?"

Now, this was over an hour after he had gotten up to use the washroom. *I guess lightweight finally woke up.* I didn't respond.

"Hello? Hey, I'm cabbing back to your area and want to say goodbye in person. I don't know your address though."

Seriously? What a doofus. I turned my phone off and went to bed. I could imagine ol' drunky drunk wandering through the streets calling my name and getting pelted with bad fruit. Good thing he was a vegan. *Not my problem. Zzzzz.*

I woke up to about five messages with the final one being, "Hey!!! I was wandering around all night looking for you. I really wish I could have said goodbye. You're so special and I'd love to take you to the champagne lounge again."

Like I'd go out with you again after that *train wreck.*

If *all* you have are veggies in your belly, it's clearly not enough to absorb copious amounts of alcohol. The lesson here is: eat meat.

JOHN #34

I pulled up to the strip mall to go to the liquor store and as I got out of my car there was a guy just getting out of his right beside me.

"Oh, hello," he said with a smile.

I just smiled and kept walking. Weren't you ever told not to talk to strangers? He was actually kind of cute, but it *was* a parking lot.

As I was strolling through the isles perusing the wine, I looked over the shelves and there he was. Our eyes met and I quickly looked away. This was kinda weird, liquor store stalking. I found my potion and got to the front checkout. Lo and behold, he had lined up right behind me. It was really awkward now. *Do I turn around? Do I tunnel vision straight ahead?*

"Nice choice," he said.

"Pardon?" I replied.

"Your wine choice. You have very good taste."

"Oh, thanks," I said as I approached the clerk. She rang me through and I started walking out a little slower than I normally would have to see if I had a follower.

Then I heard, "Nice car. You clearly have good taste in a few things."

"Well, thanks. It gets me from A to B. You have a nice little buggy too," I said.

He introduced himself, told me that he worked in the area and that he usually didn't stick around, but he was glad that he did. We started talking about music and events that were happening and he asked if I was going to a concert that night. The Johns were playing and he was friends with the lead singer. *Hmm.*

"I'm not really up too much on their music. I know their style a bit. Where are they playing?"

"At Johns' club. You should come!"

"Oh, I'm not sure, I'm going to a friend's place for dinner," I said as I held up the wine bottles for proof.

"No worries. Their set doesn't start till 10:00 pm. It would be awesome if you came."

He was very convincing. My friend wasn't a night owl, so I'd probably be leaving her place about the same time anyways.

"I'll see. It was nice to meet you," I said as I got into my car. I've met men squeezing melons in the grocery store, but the liquor store was a first.

The line up was around the block and I was second-guessing my appearance at this concert. My girlfriend had been so excited about me meeting someone that she was thrilled for me to try this new experience. Well, the wait wasn't too long and I found myself shoulder to shoulder in an intimate group of about 800 people. *He could be anywhere; I really didn't think this through.* We hadn't exchanged numbers, so this was one big crapshoot. The venue was huge and it had four different bars to choose from. *Great. This should narrow it down. If I get a shooter at every stop, that should loosen me up a bit.*

I wandered through the throngs of people to the bar closest to the stage guessing that he'd be there. I ordered a beer, 'cause that's what you do in a venue like this. I looked around at all the revelers. Everyone was having fun and the opening act was pretty good. I had a couple guys ask to buy me drinks, but I was holding out for Mr. Parking Lot.

As the main act was taking the stage, I looked towards the front and there he was! *Wow.* Finally, with all of these people, I had found him. *Hold on.* He was beside a woman and she was being very handsy with him. She looked like *way* more than a friend, that little flirt. *If he was meeting her here, why would he ask me to come?* I stood back and continued to observe this little tryst. She was still grabbing and holding onto him, but he was pretty much into the music. Still, what was I going to do? Go up to him and say, "Hey, remember me? Move over you little hoe." Not quite. So I settled in to watch the show. I ended up losing them in the crowd and that was fine with me. *Oh well, easy come, easy go.* I left before the end of the show to beat the crowd, or more like, to avoid running into him.

Fast forward a week. I was at a lounge and who walked by my table but John #34. I didn't say anything. I just let him walk by. I guess he was looking for someone because he came circling back and when he saw me, stopped dead at my table.

"Jill! Man, it is so good to see you. Hey, why didn't you come to the concert?" he asked.

"I did. I happened to see you with a very touchy female, so I just let you be," I said.

"Aww shit! That woman has been nothing but a pain in my side ever since I met her. I met her at a friend's party about a year ago and every time I see her, she thinks that she can get with me. I usually just keep going about my business and she eventually stops and moves on to another target. If I had known you were there I would have made a beeline for you. I'm so sorry about that."

Hmm. He seems genuine enough. I know I have some male friends who have been in the same situations and they just plod along. "Well, what are you gonna do to make it up to me?" I asked. "Anything you want!"

"Careful what you promise John #34."

We met up for a bite and a movie, 'cause I thought I might as well try for some balcony moves again. That night I happened to be overtired and quite giddy. So here I was, like a ten-year-old school girl, laughing at everything he said, so he felt like quite the comedic stud. Little did he know that I would laugh at a toilet plunger with the same amount of gusto that night.

We got into the movie theatre and you know how much I detest those places. Anyways, we sat down with the prerequisite popcorn and bottled water. We continued to chat until the movie started and it was a comedy so I was feeling like this just might be okay. Well, the first frame came on and I was hit with the giggles. I couldn't stop. You know when you can hardly breathe, yet you just can't stop laughing. The tears were streaming down my face and I was getting all sweaty because I couldn't stop. I was literally heaving with laughter. Now the important thing to note was that *I was the only one laughing, in the entire theatre.* Seriously. John #34 must have thought that he hit the jackpot with this hysterical laughing hyena. Good times. He just sat there smiling at me nervously throughout the movie with my laughing fits.

"Wow, I get really giddy when I'm overtired and that just hit me as ridiculously funny," I said as the lights came back on.

"I'm really glad you enjoyed it. I think the people around us had an extra appreciation for your sense of humour," he said.

Now that I was actually taking notice, quite a few people were turning around to get a look at the circus act in row 15 with mascara streaks and sweat stains.

"Well, I've never been one to care too much about what other people think and tonight, I thought that movie was hilarious."

"Well, good on you. I think it's refreshing that you are just happily yourself," he said.

He walked me to my car and we kissed and then I started laughing again.

"Sorry, I just can't seem to stop," I said.

"No worries, as long as you're not laughing at me," he said somewhat seriously.

"No! Gosh no! Sometimes when I'm overtired I just can't

stop laughing. It's a good weight loss activity too!" I said with a smile.

"Well, I'd really like to see you again. May I make you dinner?"

"Sure, that would be nice," I replied. If a guy was good with my laughing attacks, then I thought we should explore this further.

I showed up to his place on the chosen night and he had quite a nice pad—gorgeous landscaping with a huge yard and a sprawling heritage house. *Nicely done John #34.* He was so sweet. He greeted me at the door with a glass of wine and took me on a tour of his place. It was stunning, hard to believe it was all a man's taste in décor. We got to the dinner part of the date and it was a simple dish of pork medallions with mushrooms, steamed baby potatoes and carrots—my kind of meal—and it was tasty. So we talked and my laughing was kept to a normal cadence. It was pleasant, but I was seeing that there really wasn't a spark. He asked to move into the living room and filled my wine glass again. I was just about to tell him that maybe we weren't a match, but he excused himself to use the washroom. *Okay, I'll just sit down, wait until he comes back out and ease it into the conversation.*

Dude came out stark naked. I started laughing uncontrollably, like I was at the movie theatre again, only this time I was able to say, "Are you freakin' kidding me?" I put down my wine and went to get my purse.

"Hey, I thought you were giving off vibes to really connect tonight," he said now with his hands in front of his crotch.

"Uh, nope. No vibes *here* Tarzan," I said as I swung the front door open and stepped onto the deck. I just left it *wide* open, so his neighbours could get a little look-see at what John #34 was all about.

And from the looks of it, he was about three inches.

JOHN #35

Here I was minding my own business at a swanky event when all of the sudden a tall, young, and rather handsome fella came up to me and said, "If you were any more beautiful, I just couldn't take it. You are breathtaking."

Now, that's how to give a compliment. "Well, thank you," I said batting my eyelashes.

"May I buy you a drink?" he asked.

"Yes, that would be lovely. A red wine please," I responded.

It turned out that we had a few friends in common and our conversation was very lively. That could have been something to do with the intense noise in the place though. He was starting his own business, but was also working in the liquor distribution industry, which was a very handy occupation to have with me in the picture! He continued to be charming and I was getting a little swept away by his smooth talking. He asked if he could take me for dinner that week and I said yes.

Since we had friends in common I felt safe with the notion of him picking me up and he arrived promptly at 7:00 pm. He took me to a new place that his friend owned that was pretty chill with shared plates and more of a South American vibe.

Fine with me. Bring on the sangria! The conversation seemed to have changed considerably from the last time though. He was still smooth, but he wasn't pouring it on nearly as heavy as when we first met. In the other venue, it had been so lively. We were mirroring that vibe before, but now it was a little too chill (as in, pretty dull).

I was actually carrying most of the conversation, which wasn't unusual but still seemed odd recalling our last time together. I started talking to him about the charities that I was involved with and one in particular that was coming up. *I might as well make this into a* "charity ask" *meeting.* We were giving swag bags away and I thought, how fun would it be if we had single serving bottles of prosecco to give away too? Since I wasn't feeling the intense vibe anymore, and he was turning out to be more hot air than not, I thought, why not go for the ask? I would need one hundred bottles of prosecco and he agreed!

The date ended and he dropped me off. I gave him an awkward hug and followed it with, "Thanks again for dinner and committing to my charity. So when will you be able to drop the bubbly off?"

"Oh, that's it eh? Okay, well, yeah. I'll message you tomorrow and let you know," he stuttered. "Maybe I can come up for a night cap?" he then asked.

"No, this was fun, but I think things have changed with more conversation. You're a great guy but…" I tried.

"I really like you. I just know that you have had so many

more experiences than me and I know that you're older and I was kinda intimidated tonight," he said.

Aw, poor baby. Seems like Mr. Smooth just became Mr. Rocky Road. "You're a good guy. You'll find someone who is made exactly for you. Let me know about the prosecco delivery," I said as I turned to go inside.

I'm not Dr. Phil buddy. If your balls are detachable with your confidence, you might want to get that checked out.

John #36

Imagine a young Clark Kent without the glasses. Come to think of it, Clark Kent is Superman without the glasses, so why don't you just imagine Superman without the costume. Oh, but not naked! Not *yet* anyways! He had impossibly blue eyes, a strong square jaw, dark hair, a body you could bounce quarters off of, and he was a lawyer. If you were to build a man, he would be it. He started chatting me up at the gym and I welcomed the interruption—every second of it—'cause he was man candy.

He had just become a lawyer and also had some sort of proprietary thingy that he was really excited about that was bringing him passive income. He was also a wine lover and loved fitness, so we were off to a very good start. We would end up always working out at the gym together and bantering and having a really good time. One day he asked if I'd like to grab a bite after our workout and since he'd already seen me all sweaty and messy I thought, Why not?

We ended up going to a sushi place nearby and talked and talked. He was very interesting and highly intelligent; it was stimulating to speak with him. He was a really slow mover though. I mean, I knew he was into me, but he wasn't touchy and he hadn't even tried to kiss me. One thing that gave me hope was that he was free with the compliments. Even when we had first met at the gym with all of the other young tight little bouncing boobies there, he was always by my side telling me how amazing I looked. I felt very sexy with him. Even though he was considerably younger than me, he was very mature and he said he liked what I brought to the table in confidence and sensuality. *So, why hasn't he tried to kiss me yet, dammit?*

It was time to leave and as we got up to go, we ran into an old colleague who was none too subtle. "Whoa Jill, who's the hunk of meat you got there?"

"Uh, John #36," I said as I tried to walk past her in the overcrowded lobby.

"Hey, I've got a new business and I'm pretty excited about it. It's a gift basket company customizable to whatever my clients need," she said. *Well, that's only been done a hundred times before.* "Good for you," I said, still trying to get past her.

"So, John #36, what do you do?" she asked him with her eyes looking up into his dreamily.

"Oh, well, I'm uh, well, I'm a lawyer," he stammered out.

What the hell? He was always so well spoken when it was just us.

"What kind of law do you practice?" she kept on.

"Yeah, uh, it's not really people I work with. No, I mean, it's, well, I kinda work with buildings," he said.

As much as I wanted to see if he could actually carry on a conversation, I had to give the poor guy some help.

"He works mostly in real estate law. Hey, we really have to

be going. So nice to see you," I said as I finally broke free of the crowd. I got outside first and turned around to see John #36 coming out all frazzled.

"Are you okay?" I asked somewhat perplexed.

"Yeah, yeah. It's just, I'm a little shy with new people."

"How do you do with your clients though?" I asked.

"Oh, I'm actually really good with them. They come to me and I'm in my element in my office. I didn't think I was *that* bad though," he replied.

Seriously? Wow, this guy needs a dose of reality. This was a bit of a turn-off. How could a guy that was so hot and seemingly confident be so completely awkward talking with other people?

"I had a really good time Jill. You're such a good listener and I really enjoyed our conversation. Have I told you tonight how sexy you are?"

Well shit. All of a sudden the dude's found his tongue again. Maybe he was just really nervous because this was our first time out on a date. "Thanks for dinner. I guess I'll see you at the gym," I said as I turned to leave. He pulled me around and his smoldering lips met mine. *Well, that's more like it. If he got all awkward again in public, all I need to do is pull him into a lip-lock. Crisis averted.*

We were at the gym again the next night, as gym rats seem to do, and he was all jibber-jabber with no problems talking at all. *I'll take it. The more comfortable he is with me, the better he'll be when and if we go out again.* Although, I thought, I *had* to take this stallion for a test drive, even if it meant we never went anywhere in public again (besides the gym).

He had just moved into a new 30-story office building that he said was absolutely gorgeous and I had to see it. He asked if I would come with him the next night. We would pop by his office for a special vintage wine that he had and then carry on from there to dinner. Sounded good to me. It was almost as if the stammering fool from the other night was completely forgotten.

We did our workout, but not too much for me. I wanted to keep my sexy *on* more than a hosed down version of myself. We changed and then headed to his office. Now, part of me was thinking not of the mile-high club exactly, but the 30th-floor club. The thought of getting it on when you don't know if it's going to stop on a floor is sexual adrenalin! Elevator sex was on my mind and since we knew each other so well from the gym it just made sense.

We got to his building and he was such a polished gentleman, opening my door for me, giving me his arm. *Listen Superman, I want more than your arm right now, you hot piece of flesh.* It was hard to contain myself. We got into the elevator and I moved closer to him, pressing my body against his.

"Jill, there are cameras in here!" he said sharply.

"And...?" I replied with the sultriest look I could conjure.

"Well, I'm just not comfortable even kissing you in here. What if someone came in?" he said a little freaked out.

What a buzzkill, and by that, I mean "lustkill".

We got to his floor and he did a sweep of the office to see if anyone was there. At that point I just wanted some of that wine he had. He opened the bottle, poured me a glass and proceeded to take me around, explaining the architecture and the beautiful art. I felt more like I was on a real estate tour than a date. *Sheesh, how do you get the sexy back after that?*

He brought me to the last office, which was his, and it was gorgeous. The art was amazing and the view was breathtaking. He asked me to come to the window and have a closer look at the city line. I went to the window and it was truly mesmerizing. I could look at views like that every night. The lights were sparkling like thousands of diamonds and the reflection on the water was magical. All of the sudden I could feel his hardness against my hip. He had turned to face me and as I looked up at him he took my lips in his. *Okay, now we're getting somewhere.*

We became animals, ripping and tearing at each other's clothes. He had pushed me up against the window, which was kinda hot, but also kinda scary. I don't mind looking at the sites from a couple feet away from the window, but what if the window broke? Maybe my mind was too active, but I am a writer after all. It was too much for me. I maneuvered him around so he was against the window and suddenly he pushed me away. *What the hell?* He elbowed me to the side and, as I turned around all aghast, I saw that there was a security guard standing in the doorway. Presumably enjoying the show, because he had a silly-ass grin on his face.

John #36 was being more of a shield for me as he was walking towards the door, so I was able to adjust my skirt and blouse. He walked right into the guy and closed the door behind him. I couldn't hear what he was saying, but the sex vibe was dead for sure now. I went to his desk and poured more wine. Maybe that would help salvage this sexless night. I know I sound like a horny-toad, but I was *more* than ready to take it to the next level with this guy. We practically saw each other every day at the gym and I felt like we had a pretty strong connection. I sat down in one of his client chairs and turned it to face the view. *I might as well make the best of a hopeless situation.*

Half a glass of wine later, John #36 came back in apologizing profusely.

"I'm so sorry Jill. I told you I wasn't comfortable getting intimate in these types of places," he said in full blush.

"Well, if I recall, you were the one with the hard Johnson pushing up against me instigating that steamy session," I replied none too pleased.

"It was hard not to. You're so sexy."

"I'm just wondering, what did you think would happen, with you taking me to your office after hours? Didn't you think that just *maybe* we might get it on?"

"Well, I wasn't sure. I guess I kind of wanted it, but then I was nervous about the whole idea. I really just wanted you to come and see where I worked and the amazing view. I know how much you love views, so I thought it would be a romantic start to our evening," he said.

Hmmm, fair enough, I guess, but still, his awkwardness and lack of preparation, i.e. leaving the door open, was really a rookie move. Do I give this guy another chance?

"Our reservations are in half an hour, we should probably get going," he said.

Clearly, he really wasn't planning on getting it on at his office with that short of a time span anyways. *Is he just an old fashioned romantic or a non-sexual dud?* I wasn't sure if this stop-and-go personality was going to cut it for me.

"Jill? Are you okay? You seem kind of distant."

"Yeah, this just seems to be awkward with us. We get along so well at the gym and have no issues talking and having fun, but the minute we are outside of that "sweat palace", you seem to be another person John #36. I think we should just keep it as friends," I said disappointedly.

"No! I don't want to be just friends. I've never met a woman like you and I don't want to give this up. We have the potential to be magical together."

Wow, was this guy hallucinating? I mean, he was hot as hell, but his connection was so off and on. He was socially inept. Didn't he see it? It was like, when he was standing there, he was probably the most gorgeous man I had ever laid eyes on, but when it came to interaction that wasn't at the gym, he was so socially *and* sexually awkward. It's almost like a beautifully decadent truffled "mac 'n' cheese" that your friend says they're going to make you and they give you a serving and it's just cauliflower minced up with tofu curds. *The hells' up with that?*

I'll pass thanks. (But we would take such good photos together…)

John(ette) #37

Well, if that doesn't get you wondering…

I went to one of my favourite places, just like Cheers (where everybody knows your name), and saddled up to the bar. Wouldn't cha know it, I made friends right away. There was a man and woman, and my first thought and instinct was that he was gay and she was fabulous. Turned out he was not gay and she was not fabulous, but their friends who came *over* were absolutely fabulous!

The angels from the other side of the room came to my rescue and we started chatting. They were so full of life (and wine) and love (and wine) and laughter (and wine) that I just *had* to join them at their table at their request. They wanted to know *all* about me and were so lovely. There were three of them and they were all mothers of varying ages of children, but still had their wits about them. Johnette seemed to be a leeeeetle more touchy than the others, but we were all girls and that's what girls do. We carried on and on and were having a lovely time AND THEN JOHN #23 SAT AT THE TABLE NEXT TO US. *Let the games begin!* After all, I was a few glasses in by now.

"Hey buddy, how are ya?" I asked.

"Oh, hey Jill, pretty good," he replied very sheepishly.

Remember this was the dude that tried to recycle his ex. "How's the ex? Is she a present tense now?"

"Um, no, that didn't work out."

"Oh, imagine that," I said with an Elvis lip snarl.

"Yeah, that should have never happened, I'm so sorry," he retorted.

"No worries, I've moved on. I gotta say though that our sex was pretty animal…at the time," I said as I returned my focus to my gaggle of girls.

"Oh Jill, who was that?" Johnette asked with her hand on my back.

"Oh, just an old buddy that I hung around with for a bit." *Shit, I really was becoming a dude.*

We kept talking and laughing and Johnette was all about me, touching and complimenting me. I didn't think anything about it until the server came by and asked if we would like any more beverages. I said no and turned to Johnette and she planted a wet one right on my lips.

"Yes please! We would like two more reds please," she said.

I was dumbfounded. I literally didn't know what to say or do and that NEVER happens. Okay, almost never. *Anyways, what the hell was that? My experimental days are waaay over.* I looked to our table companions and they hadn't noticed a thing. I looked back at kissy lips and said, "That was weird."

"Oh, I'm sorry. You're just so beautiful and your lips are so welcoming," she replied.

"Well, I'm not gay and I'm not interested in pursuing anything physical with you," I said.

"Okay, I just acted on impulse. Can we just forget that happened?" she said.

Kinda hard now lady. I continued kibitzing with the ladies across the table and then called it a night.

I went outside to hail a taxi and kissy lips came out and said, "Hey, I really am sorry about that inside. I shouldn't have done that."

Just then the taxi pulled up. "Do you mind if I come with you? I heard you say what area you lived in and I'm just another few blocks away," she asked.

What the hell? If she tried anything again, I would just throat punch her Ronda Rousey style.

We got in front of my place and I said, "Goodnight, it was nice to meet you."

"Can I come in?"

Haven't you ever heard of 'no means no'?!? I just looked at her, aghast. Now, I don't *usually* use the word aghast, but when I do, I'm struck with overwhelming shock or amazement. Was it flattering being hit on by a beautiful woman? A little. Did I like the kiss? A little. But bottom line is, I like sausage.

Hey, maybe she should meet that tattoo-headed lady

hanging around at that vegetarian place at 12th and Lesbian. No sausage allowed there. He-he-he...

John #38

They say that music soothes the soul, so I went in search of some soothing at one of the hotel lounges with a piano bar. The vibe was fun. Everyone dressed to impress and were sipping the cocktail concoctions that the hottie mixologist had come up with for the night. He must chuckle at what people are willing to pay for—whatever he deems on point for the moment. Seriously, you can buy a *bottle* for the price of some of those drinks. *What do I care? My drinks are usually bought for me.* Oh, and right on cue, the server brought over a glass of wine from the lovely fellow at the bar. Well, he was quite the looker, a little older but with a certain *je ne sais quoi* about him (the French always have a sexier way of saying things, *oui?*).

I held my glass up to accept the drink and cheers him. He did the same and then came over to my highboy table.

"You are absolutely stunning," he said with a glint in his eye.

"Well, thank you kind sir," I replied.

"I'm in town from Oregon for a few days. Perhaps you have a few pointers of what I should see." "It depends on what kind of activities you like. I've got some sightseeing, shopping, eating and hot spots to share if you'd like."

"I'd like to share this table with *you* right now, if that's okay," he said.

Oooo, smooth talker. "But of course," I said with a smile. It felt very James Bondishy. I'm sure that Daniel Craig would like it being described that way: "Cheerio then. Let's go to that 'Bondishy' kind of place."

Anyways, the night was fabulous. His friend ended up joining us when he got to the hotel and that was okay with me. Two very attractive men were treating me doubly fine. Now the dilemma was, which one should I choose? The first guy had dark hair, blue eyes and was more on the polished side, while the second guy was dirty blonde, green eyes and had more of a rugged look. *Hmmm, decisions, decisions.* "Jill, are you still with us?" asked John #38.

"Yes, of course, just lost in a thought. So, where do you think you're going tomorrow?"

"We were thinking of heading to Granville Island Market. It sounded wonderful when you described it. Will you please join us?" John #38 asked.

"Well, I've got some clients to see in the morning but could squeeze away around 2:00 pm," I said.

"I'd like to squeeze you, you beautiful creature!" he said with a wink. Dirty blonde spoke up just then, saying, "I'm heading to bed, I'll catch you in the morning, bud, and I'll see you tomorrow afternoon Jill."

"G'night buddy. Jill, may I buy you dessert at the bistro?" John #38 asked. *Well, I don't really eat desserts, but I could certainly take a bite of this delicious morsel of manliness right now.* "That would be lovely," I replied. So I guess my decision was made for me, which was just fine. John #38 was more commanding and called the shots and that was one very sexy trait.

We got to the very quaint little bistro. He ordered a *crème brûlée* to share and an espresso. I opted for a decaf as I settled into the cozy booth. He was so sweet and interesting and he had a lot of funny stories to share. I was really digging this guy. As time went on I found myself thinking about living in Oregon, meeting his grown daughters, living the life of luxury. I could probably get him to move to California 'cause it was only one state away after all and I really did enjoy the sunshine more. But, time would tell now wouldn't it.

At risk of *this* Cinderella turning into a pumpkin at midnight, I bid my American Prince Charming *adieu* (Ooo, la, la, look at me and my French still!). With a kiss on my cheek and a hail of a taxi, I was off.

When the next day came around, I was on cloud nine, drifting in and out of my new fantasy world. Time came to meet and I was floating on air. John #38 was there and he greeted me with a warm kiss on my cheek and an all-enveloping hug. *Mmm, I love being enveloped.* His buddy was going to join us a bit later, so we started to stroll along and I was showing him all things Vancouver in the market. We were feeding each other delicious morsels and being that couple that people despise and envy at the same time.

"I'd like to kiss you," he said as he turned my body to face his.

Oh dear god in heaven, I was melting. He released me, took my hand again and we kept walking. I was grinning ear to ear like Jimmy Fallon does whenever Justin Timberlake comes on his show (now, *that's* a bromance!).

We wandered aimlessly, kissed, hugged, and ate a little more. This was truly an awesome date! We were standing looking at the beautiful water view when all of the sudden I was picked up from behind. I was just about to scream, not sure whether I was going to be thrown into the water by some crazed person. Then I turned to see it was John #38's friend. Good thing for him I didn't have my hand on my switchblade. *Dumbass.*

"You scared the crap out of me!" I yelled at him.

"Haha. Sorry! You guys were looking so quaint together, I had to jostle it up a little bit," he replied.

"Maybe a little notice next time buddy," Prince Charming said with some authority.

"Yeah, okay. So you guys ready for some food?" buddy asked.

John #38 looked at me.

"I could do with some wine," I replied.

We walked up to the outdoor patio and got a seat with a beautiful view. It was like we had known each other for ages. John #38 was still the perfect gentleman and buddy was like his bratty little brother. *Whew, I scored the good one there!*

Our afternoon became early evening and they said that they planned to extend their stay and go up to Whistler. They were leaving tomorrow for the mountain.

"I would love it if you would join us," John #38 said.

Hmmm, I've kinda been in this situation before and it didn't turn out so good. "I'm not sure about that. I still really don't know you. I mean, it *feels* like I've known you for a long time, but I really don't." "I understand, maybe we can work something out for you to be comfortable. Of course I'd be more than happy to get you your own room and I'll take care of it," John #38 said.

Well, it did sound tempting, but I also had to meet with some clients tomorrow. Hey, maybe that was better because I'd be bringing up my own car. I could come and go as I liked. Well, living on the edge, I said, "Sounds good! I'll be up in the late afternoon. So, you'll have it all worked out by the time I get there?"

"Yes darling. I'll text you your confirmation just in case we're not in our rooms when you get there. This is going to be great!" John #38 replied.

We carried on the evening at the restaurant and were all having a fabulous time. This was how life should be—great connections, laughter, flirting and wine, lots of wine, of course. Time came for me to go home and John #38 came down with me and nuzzled with me in the alcove. *Hot, hot, hot.* He really was reminiscent of the old rat pack guys that you see in the movies and I was eating it up.

Morning came early and so did my client meetings. I got things out of the way as soon as possible. You could call it speed dealing, but I got that shit done. I got a text from him with my room confirmation. *Whistler, here I come!*

I texted him when I got into the village to let him know that I had arrived. By the time I got to the front desk, I still hadn't heard back from him. *Maybe they're in the pool or something.* I got the fob to my room and went up to put my bag there. I texted John #38 again, nothing. I went to his door and knocked, nothing. Just as I was turning around to go back to my room he came to the door.

"Hey beautiful, sorry about that, I was having a little nap."

What, are you 95 years old or something? "Oh, well, I didn't mean to interrupt you gramps," I said sarcastically.

He put his arms around me and said, "Now, you lil' whipper-snapper, some of us old guys need to recharge when we hang out with an energizer bunny like you!"

"Haha, okay, fair enough. You need more time?" I asked.

"Well, why don't you join me for a little cuddle time before we head out?"

I had just come up on a white knuckle, winding, slippery road, so I didn't need a sleep; I needed a drink. Besides, it was a little too soon for a "cuddle time" with John #38.

"Nah, I'll pass. Why don't you just meet me down in the bar when you're ready," I said.

"It's no fun to drink alone," he said.

Well, clearly, he doesn't know me very well. "I'll be fine. How long you going to be snoozing?" "Well, I don't want you to drink alone and I certainly don't want any playboys trying to pick you up. I'm going to jump in the shower and be down in 15," he said as he planted a sensual wet one on me.

I turned to go and he smacked me on the ass and said, "Don't you dare pay for anything. Make sure that you tell them to put it on the room gorgeous."

Was there any doubt? "Sounds good. See you in a bit."

I ordered a beautiful red that was so full and rich it made me swirl my tongue in my mouth. *That brings to mind other things that make me swirl my tongue in my mouth...* Just then, I felt a hand on my shoulder and a kiss to my cheek. *Aw, my American Prince Charming.* I turned.

"Holy hell!" I yelled as buddy stood there with a bouquet of flowers.

"These are for you gorgeous," buddy said as he placed the flowers in my lap.

What the hell?

"I know that you and John #38 are starting something special, but I just had to get these for you," he said.

"Kinda inappropriate, don't cha think?" I said.

"Nope. Just because you two are hitting it off doesn't mean that I can't get you some beautiful flowers. I think that you should be able to appreciate people and show them with nice gestures like this." "Have you ever heard the story of Cain and Abel? It didn't end well," I replied.

We just stared at each other.

"Hello you beautiful creature you!" John #38 said as he leaned over and gave me a kiss. I looked wide-eyed at buddy. "Wow, those are gorgeous flowers. Where did you get them?"

"Um, buddy just gave them to me," I said as I sat there dumbfounded.

"Hey man, I'm not looking to mow your grass, I just thought that Jill deserved some flowers," buddy replied.

"And here I was concerned that some *other* playboy was trying sweep her off her feet, but *you* man? Not cool," John #38 said.

Well, he was very composed for the situation; then again, what would violence solve?

"John #38, c'mon bud. You know that I'm not trying to move in on you," he tried.

"Oh, just like the situation with Melanie, eh?" John #38 responded.

"Well, that was just blown out of proportion," buddy said.

"So you're still trying to make me believe that you just showed up at her girls' night at the hotel lounge coincidentally? And then bought a couple of rooms so the ladies wouldn't have to worry about getting home safely. And *then* you showed up with champagne? Fuck off. Consider this friendship over." I looked up at John #38.

"C'mon Jill. Let's get out of this place. It's beginning to really stink in here," John #38 said.

I still had the flowers in my lap and when I stood up John #38 took them from me and put them over on the bar.

But, they were so pretty...

"I've had enough of that douche bag's shenanigans. Sorry that you had to be a part of that," he said as we walked into a restaurant.

"Did he try to move in on your dates a lot?" I asked.

"This was one time too many. I've known him for about five years and he wasn't always that way. He's a good guy under it all. That's why I've let it slide. It's like he's my little brother and he gets competitive with me. He never seems to get his own date, always wants to try to move in on mine." "What ended up happening with Melanie?" I asked.

"Oh, her. Well, I can't just blame buddy on that one. It turned out that she was pretty welcoming with his come-ons and pretty welcoming to his cock that night he showed up."

"Oh, I'm sorry that happened. That sucks," I said sympathetically.

"Well, it takes two, so I let the Bro Code rule on that one because I didn't know the whole story at first, unfortunately. Enough is enough though. Buddy's on his own now," John #38 said.

"What if we run into him tonight?" I asked.

"I'm a big boy, I'll be okay. How about you?" he said.

"It'll just be weird, I guess," I replied.

We sat at dinner in a bit of a purgatory—nothing amazing and nothing hellish, just meh. After dinner, he asked if I wanted to get a night-cap and it didn't really make sense. Here I had what seemed like a really nice guy who had just ended a friendship and even though he was a man, still had some emotion attached to it.

"It doesn't feel like that's a good idea. You seem to still be bummed, which is totally understandable," I said.

"I'm sorry that I've let it affect me. I guess I knew that someday this would happen, but I was hoping that he would just grow up. It would really mean a lot to me if you and I could just chill out and talk a little more—about us, not him."

"Okay, can we go to the other bar though, to minimize the risk of running into him?" I asked.

"Of course, beautiful. I want to show you that I'm here for you and not the stupid shit that happened earlier."

We walked into the bar and the coast was clear. It was pretty busy, but we scored a table in the corner to keep our backs against the wall and our eyes forward.

All of a sudden, we found our groove again. Looking into his gorgeous blue eyes, I was completely drawn in. Yeah, it could have been the wine, but I just couldn't stop myself and I went in for the kiss. I took his lips in mine with my hand on his strong jaw. *Gawd, he was delicious.* I pulled back to gaze into his dreamy blueness again. His eyes went wide! *What?* He shot out of his seat like a rocket. *What the...* there was buddy.

"Get out of here," John #38 said to him.

"It's a free world dude. Chill out," replied buddy.

"I won't fucking chill out until you check out, you fucking asshole."

"Whoa, I've never seen you like this dude. It was just a

misundersta…" buddy tried as John #38 grabbed him by the collar and pushed him through the patio doors.

Shit! What should I do? Go and see what the hell's going on or stay here. Shit. I heard some of the furniture being rearranged outside and not in a "Designer Guys" kind of way. I looked at the bartender. Both of our eyes went big. This wasn't the type of place that you would think a fight would break out. I mean, it wasn't Buffalo Bills or anything like that. I got up and just then John #38 came back in with his jacket ripped.

"Are you okay?" I asked as I reached out to him. *I gotta admit, this was kinda hot, literally being fought for, like in the old days when they would duel for the heart of the fair maiden. Okay, admittedly, no-one would use those words to describe me. I'm more of a slightly loose, kissing bandit of a woman that has a fierce temper when she's hungry.*

"What happened?" I asked.

"Buddy's leaving now. He's just getting his things and getting a taxi back to Vancouver. He'll no longer be a thorn in our sides," he said as he pulled me into his arms.

His lips were so juicy and sensual. *Oh dear god, I wanted him and I wanted him bad.* This was not good. I only had the tiniest amount of common sense left; between the wine, and Prince Charming fighting for my love, it was almost too much. I sat back down. As I continued to gaze into his eyes I realized that they were starting to get fuzzy. I even did the one eye squint to get him in focus. *Not good. Nuts!* This had to end now; otherwise I would be a stumbling fool.

"Are you okay beautiful? You seem kinda off," he said.

"Need my bed now," I blurted out, only like a drunky-drunk person can.

"Let's get you up to your room. This has been way too much excitement for one night," he said as he scooped me into his strong ribcage. *Mmmm ribs. I'm hungry.*

I woke up with a booming headache. Now, when I say booming, I don't mean like a nice little base being played; I mean like Russel Crowe not getting his way in a hotel. It was bad. I looked at my phone. It was after 10:00 am. *Shit, when's check-out?* There was a text from John #38 asking me to call him when I was up. *When the room stops spinning, I'll do my best. Shit.* This was not good. I hadn't been this hungover since grade eight, puking up with Carrie in the walkway by our junior high school.

"Room service," I heard from the door.

Shit.

I slowly got up and half crawled towards the door, saying hoarsely, "Leave it there please."

"Will do. Thank you miss," was the reply.

Well, I got as far as the chair by the door and just sat there. I don't know how long it was because I dozed off again and then heard another knock.

"Hey babe, you okay in there?" came John #38's voice.

Oh, such a sweet man. Crap, I must look like shit right now. I can't let him see me like this. Right then the door opened. I had forgotten that he had my key from when he let me in last night.

"Babe, you don't look so good," he said with far too much compassion for a drunken dame. "Yeah, well, I feel like crap."

He pulled in the room service cart with a beautiful bouquet of red roses that were from him, orange juice, a carafe of coffee and some scones. *Good lord, food will not be passing my lips for any of the foreseeable near future.*

"Have some orange juice. It will help to balance you out," he said as he poured me a glass. I took a small sip and it seemed to be okay, abiding in my digestive tract, then slowly draining into my stomach. I smiled weakly. "Thanks, this is all very sweet of you. How did you sleep?" I asked.

"Oh, you didn't hear anything last night? Buddy came by my room drunker than a skunk and was trying to break down my door. Security came and kicked his ass out. It was quite a scene. I'm surprised you didn't hear it. You must be a really heavy sleeper," he said.

Not a heavy sleeper, but apparently a very heavy drinker last night and had passed out to the world.

"It must have been the wine," I said with a shrug.

"When's check-out?" I asked, praying that we had a late checkout.

"Actually, I got us the rooms for another night. That's if you want to. I know that last night wasn't what either of us expected, so I thought if we had one more night we could make it our own thing. What do you say?"

"Umm, well, I don't have any meetings tomorrow."

"Then it's settled. Let me get you into the spa and they'll have you feeling like a million bucks!" *I'd be okay with feeling like 50 cents right about now.*

The spa was amazing! It was so exhilarating and refreshing, *exactly* what I needed. The unfortunate attendants though, they never knew what hit them when my pores started oozing all of the alcohol out of my system. Even I was crinkling my nose from all of the fermented grapes and whatever vodka's made with. It wasn't pretty, but they were making *me* pretty, so that was all that mattered.

"Well, hello there! I see you're feeling much better beautiful! I can actually see a sparkle in your eyes," he said, as he pulled me in for a kiss in the lobby.

Mmm, this is the life, being spoiled, kissed and adored. I am loving this.

"What would you like to do now?" I asked my American Prince Charming.

"How about a little shopping, my treat."

"You don't need you to do that," I said out loud when my mind was saying, *Hell yeah!*

"Jill, you've been through a lot and have been such a good sport. Please let me treat you. I won't take no for an answer," he said adamantly.

Whew! I was so glad that he trumped my response with common sense.

"Oh, it's so sparkly and expensive. I don't think I could," I said through batted eyelashes in the jewelry store. *Please, please, please, it's so beautiful and it looks so pretty on my finger*, I was willing my thoughts to him with all of my power.

"She'll have that wrapped up with a bow please," John #38 said.

Well, if Prince Charming keeps up with this, he's gonna get a lot more than my glass slipper tonight.

We canoodled, kissed, strolled, stopped for wine (I'm not sure how my liver was able to do it again, but she deserved a raise) and I was pretty much having the time of my life. He talked about his two grown girls that were the lights of his life and how he was developing a couple new businesses. I absolutely love it when a man talks to me about how he's going to make more money. I love money—er, I mean, I love it when he follows his dream and fulfills his passion. *Whatevs, as long as I keep getting some sparkly things.*

Dinner was extravagant. I'm talking about champagne from the special cellar, beluga caviar from the Caspian Sea, and dinner from—well I'm not sure. It was lamb, so it could have been from New Zealand or perhaps Michael Jackson's vacant Neverland ranch. Either way, it was DELISH. I was ready for these clothes to come off, now. *Okay, maybe I'll wait until after dinner at least. Hmm, come to think of it, do I think this guy is dating material or just a weekend tryst? Should I give him access to my lady bits tonight, or should I see where this was going to go in the long term? What a dilemma.*

"Jill, are you okay?" John #38 said, interrupting my thoughts.

"Hey, yes, all good. Dinner was absolutely amazing! Thank you!"

"What do you say we go for a cigar and a scotch?" he said.

"Sounds good to me!" I said like a teacher starting summer holidays. *Wait a minute, where are you allowed to smoke cigars anymore?*

We got to the restaurant and, after a private conversation with the *maître d'*, we were set up all by ourselves on the patio. *Heaven.* It was winter weather and we were on a heated patio having a gorgeous body-warming scotch and a decadent cigar. This was definitely my kind of man, making this kind of magic happen. Our server was uber attentive without being a nuisance. He even did a run to the cigar store for us, lovely soul. Our night under the stars, feeling our breath in the cold, sipping deliciousness and having his hands on me was everything it sounded like—fabulousness times two.

I'm not sure if I learned a lesson from the previous night or hadn't drunk as much, but I was feeling fairly lucid when John #38 said, "Hey beautiful, I really like you and I don't want this to be just a fling. I want to see where this can go beyond this time away. I've never been with someone who makes me feel so alive and so free. I'm not sure if you want to come to my suite or go to your room, but either way, I want to continue this beyond tonight. You will love Oregon and I can't wait for you to meet my daughters."

Okay, question answered. But what to do? I am an adult after all. I could very justifiably ride this man all night and make him scream for more, or just go to my room. Damn. Let's see if his words really do ring true.

"I think that I need to go to my room tonight," I said and immediately thought of that commercial where there's that little girl with the training undies saying 'I'm a big girl now'. *Who would have thought?*

I awoke the next day to a beautiful note under my door: Jill, you are my princess and I can't wait to bring you to my kingdom and share my life with you.

Well, if that don't make you go "shiiiit", I don't know what does.

Spring forward two weeks when I got into my car and started the drive to Oregon. The last time I was there was with an ex and I bailed with a bike coming down a hill at the Gorge. I'm still sporting that divot in my leg. Anyways, the excitement was crazy, mounting up for two weeks and then the drive when he kept on texting me (I only looked when I was stopped, or when I was going along the highway with *no one* around, honest!).

I pulled up to his estate and my mouth fell open. Wow, this guy really *was* loaded. He greeted me at the door with a smile and a chocolate cake. Okay, remember, I'm not much for sweets, but this was a noble effort.

"Hey gorgeous! Welcome to Casa John #38. Your wish is my command," he said before he devoured my lips in his.

Mmm, after that long drive I was ready for another kind of meat, and it didn't need to be cooked...

After I put my clothes back on and walked into the kitchen, he presented me with a generous glass of vino. *Bless him.* We talked about the week and my drive and what we were going to do for the next couple of days. I was pretty stoked. He toured me around his estate and, I must say, it was pretty impressive, except for the pictures of his exes. *What is it with some guys? Oh well, he doesn't owe me any changes, yet.*

The next morning came and he was bright and cheery as he brought me coffee in bed. I felt so spoiled. So, the plan was to go to see one of his daughters where she was a cheer-leading coach (pretty foreign to this Canadian, but I had heard of these things), maybe go for lunch with her and then head to a dinner boat cruise. We got to the field and were in the stands looking at the rehearsal of the little ones cheering and it was so cute. I noticed though that John #38 wasn't as touchy as he had been every time we had seen each other. *Flag.* I knew that I was going to meet one of his daughters and he might be nervous, but really? *Not good.*

I focused on the cheer team again. They were ten-year-olds and we all know how cute that can be. The practice was finally over and we walked singly down the steps to the field.

"Baby girl, this is my *friend* Jill," John #38 said.

No. No, this is not cool. I know I'm not your girlfriend, but I drove over six hours and we have spent some pretty amazing time together. At the least, I'm just Jill, not your "friend" Jill.

"So nice to meet you Jill. Hey Daddy, Jeremy is coming to pick me up because it's his mom's birthday. Can I see you after the weekend?"

Okay, I guess that plan was made then—no lunch with the daughter.

We walked back to his car sans any physical contact whatsoever. When we got into the car I said, "Hey, so why the hands off approach with me today?"

"What? Really? You thought I was inattentive?" he replied.

"Uh, yeah, I did. You have been very demonstrative since we met and then today, you treated me like an ugly stepsister. No handholding, no touching, no kissing, and the way you introduced me was a little cold. You could have just said Jill and not put me in the 'friend' category."

"Wow, I had no idea. I'm so sorry," he replied.

How could he have not known that his pattern with me completely changed? I called BS. The drive back to his place wasn't filled with all of the lovey, lusty bits from before, and I really wasn't sure what to do. He had invited me to come and visit him *and* meet his daughter and then turned out to be all platonic. This wasn't going to be for me. I could still drive home because I hadn't had anything to drink yet. *I know that was a miracle in itself.*

We got back to his place and he said, "Jill, look, I am so sorry. It's just that I haven't really introduced anyone to my daughter since I split with her mother, and that was over ten years ago. This was more awkward than I wanted it to be and I'm so sorry."

Damn it. Why couldn't this be easy with these Johns? Do I believe or do I doubt?

"Please let me take you out tonight to show you how much I really care about you. I want to shout from the treetops that you're with me! I really do," he said with the cutest most convincing smile. *Shit.* "Well, as long as I'm put first then I'll go," I said with an unsettling *déjà vu* lurking in my head.

I put on my very sultry dress that was classy yet screamed sex. Nobody puts baby in the corner. We got to the boat and it wasn't what I had anticipated. There were undesirables there. In fact, they were everywhere. *Ewww.* It was a charity event and there were silent auction tables, so we grabbed some wine and started making the rounds. John #38 was still acting weird and aloof and the whole event just seemed too put on and too awkward. I wasn't going to have any of it.

The captain came up and started trying to amp his flirt with me.

"So, what's a gorgeous girl like you doing on a dingy like this?" he asked. "He brought me, and I had no idea I needed a paddle," I answered as I pointed to John #38.

"Ooo honey, you got some spirit, I like that. How 'bout we get some photos?" the captain asked. *What the hell.* "Fine by me," I said. We sat down as the photographer came to us and I was making the best of this situation. The pics turned out fabulously and then John #38 came up and asked how everything was.

"Good thanks. How are you doing?"

"Oh, pretty good. A lot of people here I know, so it's kinda like a fish bowl," he replied.

What the hell? He was the one who chose this fish bowl and had to know he would run into people that he knew. What was the big deal? Oh shit, was he married?

"Hey, John #38, are you married?" I blurted out.

"What? God no. I told you. It's just different for me. I told you I haven't dated openly in forever and this is a pretty big deal for me."

"Well, it's weird for me when you start off all cozy in Vancouver and now in your 'hood you're all cold. It's not cool with me, no pun intended," I said.

"I don't know what to say Jill. I really like you, but I guess my actions seem a little cooler here," he replied.

Not gonna work for me, but I wasn't about to head home after eight at night and with wine in my belly.

"Let's make the best of the night and go from there," I said.

The dance floor lit up and one of the ship hands tried to light it up with me on the dance floor. *Uh, no.* So then, awkward became "get me out of here" and eventually we went back to John #38's place. It was a cold night at the estate, if you know what I mean. Daylight came and I quietly got up and proceeded to gather my pre-packed bags.

"Hey, whatcha doing?" John #38 asked.

"Oh, going to get a jump on the traffic back home."

"Jill, it's Sunday, there is no traffic."

"Look, it's clear you're not ready for a relationship."

"But…"

"No, if you can't be the same as you are with me in Vancouver, then clearly this won't work for me. It's a shame, really," I said as I grabbed my CFM shoes from the previous night and headed towards the door.

"That's it?" he asked.

"Yup, pretty much."

When I make up my mind, it's set in stone and so is my heart.

"Thanks for your hospitality," I said as I opened the front door.

I left the door open as I put my bag in the back and started my car. I briefly looked in the rearview to see John #38 looking quite distraught. *Oh well.*

"A hundred bottles of beer on the wall, a hundred bottles of beer," I started singing as I started my long trek back home. *Don't ever confuse a frog with Prince Charming 'cause not all frogs turn into real princes. C'est la vie. Crap, here I am again with the French! Mmm, French food means Frog legs and they taste just like chicken. I'm hungry again.*

John #39

I'm just a girl standing in front of a (multitude of) boy(s) asking him to love her. Oh, is that a line from a movie? Well, I'm borrowing it. After my long run of dating, I thought I would take a pause and go a little harder at the gym with my buddy John #39. If I can't make sweet love, I'll make sweet muscle.

We had known each other for about three years and usually worked out at least a couple nights a week together. It was such a simple and easy friendship. He was a handsome enough guy, but just too awkward and geeky for me. After our workouts or hikes we'd often go back to his place and either make some dinner or order in.

We'd talk about *everything*, and I mean *everything*. It was so comfortable with him that sometimes we'd even give each other (fully-clothed) massages after some of our heavy workouts. It was just our thing. He would usually run the bath for himself after dinner because he knew that I would only be staying to finish my wine and then vamoose. It was just so no-stress. If I had too much wine to drink on a weekend he'd let me have his loft and he'd sleep downstairs on the couch. It didn't hurt that he would always make me fresh squeezed juice and a delicious breakfast. Ooo, I can see how this is sounding now. Maybe I should have seen the signs. But, I had even brought a couple of dates to his place to hang out and there was nothing from him. No moves, no comments, nothing. Friend-zone.

One night we were going to a box seat with a friend's company to see Lenny Kravitz. I thought John #39 could stand to meet some new people, i.e. women, and there would be a lot there, so I invited him. I would arrive at his place as per the norm for a glass of vino and then we'd take a taxi downtown.

John #39 was acting weird. I couldn't quite place my finger on it, but it was like he was laughing louder at my jokes, giving me more compliments than normal and being far more touchy than he had ever been. Maybe he was just all giddy to see Lenny. Hey, guys can get that way too you know.

We went for dinner first at a rather fancy-schmancy place and he was beaming the entire time. We had such a good rapport and a very witty banter with each other. Everywhere we went, people were always drawn to us. Fun buddies and all that, you know? This night though, the server whom we had been having a really fun time with said, "You two are the best couple that I've ever seen. You're so in tune with each other. How long…"

"We're not together!" I blurted out a little too loudly and a little too harshly. "I mean, we're just friends," I said as I tried to soften it.

John #39's face drooped like Mick Jagger's. It was sad.

Oh, well, we're going to be seeing Lenny in a short bit. Buck up, you ol' sausage. Listen, he'd never *ever* said that he was interested in dating me and I was *so* not interested in *ever* dating him, so we were to stay friends. So, he paid the bill, as he always did, and—*hey, wait a minute, was that another sign that he liked me more than a friend? Nah! Just friends 'til the end.*

We got to the concert and I went to my friend to tell her that John #39 was acting kind of strange. I asked if she saw it too. Only thing was, she had only met him once at more of a corporate event, so she didn't really have any gauge of his level of normal.

The concert started and it was AMAZING. I mean, it was LENNY!!! We were all singing and dancing and having lots of wine. I kept my little body moving and circulating and put the oddness of John #39 out of my mind. It was an awesome night.

After the concert when we were in the taxi on the way back to his place, he asked me to come up for a glass of wine. Now this was usually a very normal occurrence for us. More often than not, we would go back to his place and recap, much like one would do with a girlfriend. But, wait, not a boy and girl "girlfriend". Girl "girlfriend" to girl "girlfriend". You know what I mean.

"I think I'll just continue on in the taxi."

"Jill, we *always* recap and that was such a fun night. You *have* to come up for a glass of vino," he pleaded with his puppy dog eyes.

Crap. Oh well, maybe this weirdness was just all in my mind anyways.

"Okay, I hope you have that delish Barolo wine, dude," I said.

We got up to his place and he whipped out some charcuterie and a glass of that beautifully deep Barolo for us. We were falling right back into the olden days, you know, like Tuesday when we were buddies with no weirdness. I had dropped my defenses and in my mind welcomed my old *friend* back. *I was just overthinking things earlier I guess. He really is a funny guy, so sweet. I hope he finds himself a good woman one of these days. Hey, maybe I'll be the "grooms-maid". Ha! That would be so fun. Hey, where did John #39 go?* I was so in my mind and he's such a putterer that I finally noticed he had just come back from turning his bath water on. *Oh, he's right on cue. I'm almost finished my wine, so that means a bath for him and a taxi home for me.* I stood up to get my phone from my purse to call a taxi. "Jill. Would you like to have a bath with me?" he asked, as he approached me in the hallway. *Whaaa? Shit. What? Shit.*

Shit. Shit. Shit.

"Uh. Um. Well. Geez. That. Um. I can't. I mean, I, wow. Just, wow. John #39, no," I stuttered, as I got my purse and made a beeline for the door.

I started walking home, not the best idea as he lived in an "up and coming" area that was right beside commercial buildings. It was just me, a few homeless people and then some hookers (once I went a few blocks up and turned the corner).

What the hell? Now I was getting mad. *How dare he? I mean, he had all this time. We've been hanging out for three years and he's never even made a move on me. He's never said that he's interested. Shit, if he had told me from the get-go, this disturbingly awkward situation could have been totally avoided, or at least dealt with way back then. Shit.*

He messaged the next day to say that we needed to talk. *No shit Sherlock.* He agreed to come to my place and we'd try to have a normal conversation about it to see if we could salvage this friendship.

"Hey. So, how are you?" he asked sheepishly.

"First of all I was weirded out and then I was pissed. Seriously dude, how could you throw away our friendship? You've never once told me that you were interested," I replied.

"Well, to be fair to me, you're always dating one guy or another and I just never felt like I had an opening."

"That's BS. We hang out *all* the time! You think that you could have mentioned it at the beginning?"

"I was too intimidated by you. When we met at the gym you just knew everyone. You had such confidence and I just was happy that you gave me the time of day. Then when you gave me a few pointers and we started working out together, you were dating a couple different guys so..." he tried.

"So what? Seriously John #39, I really feel like I've been hit in the stomach. I love you as a friend, and nothing more. I just don't think we can go backwards from this. Listen, it sucks that we have different feelings for one another. You know it would never work with us. I'm way too much for you, too high maintenance. Anyways, there's a cute little lady out there just waiting for you to squeeze her some orange juice," I said, as it finally clicked in my head.

Ladies, if your heterosexual male friend always pays, massages you, and squeezes your hung-over ass fresh OJ, he's into you.

Shit. Maybe if there was champagne with the OJ, I could have tried…uh, nope.

JOHN #40

Now I *really* needed to wipe the cooties off of me and get an honest-to-goodness lust connection. I headed out to one of the sports bars with a friend, which was something we rarely did (leave that to the cheerleader types, you know). This one night, though, I was throwing all caution to the wind and going to a sausage fest.

There was a medical convention *and* a football game on, so there was bound to be a score. (Like what I did there?) We got to the bar and wandered up to the pool tables. Yes, it truly was *that* kind of bar. Listen, desperate times call for desperate measures. We circled the table and were just on our way back down the stairs when I heard, "You're not going to stay for a game?" coming from an arrestingly handsome man with a burn scar on the entire left side of his face.

There was something about his confidence, his body, and his eyes, that I didn't even focus on the scar.

"I didn't think that there was any competition up here, so thought I'd come back later," I replied. "Ooo, a fiery one! Well, if m'lady would like to partner with little ol' me and maybe show me a few pointers, I would be most grateful," he said.

Hmmm. I looked at my girlfriend. She shrugged.

"Any money on this game?" I asked as I got a stick.

"Haha! You really are something! These are some colleagues I just met in town for the weekend conference, so we're pretty chill," he said.

Little did he know that I didn't really play. Usually after the first few shots I lose interest and focus and—oh look, shiny things.

"No money on it, but how about we bet them a round?"

"Okay by me," I responded. I hoped like hell that he knew how to play.

Crack. The other team broke and sunk one. *No biggie.* I went to the other end of the table and proceeded to lean over the table and have a really good look at the balls…on the table. Ooops, were those my boobs almost cascading right out of my top? Oh darn, you missed. It was my partner's turn now.

"Honey, you're used to sinking things into tight spaces. You can do it," I said with a wink. *Who the hell was I becoming?* All I needed were ripped fishnets and a cigarette hanging out of my mouth.

John #40 turned out to be a shark. He sunk the rest and the poor boobs (not mine) had to buy us a round. We sat in a back corner and things started to get real. He told me about how he got the scar and that it apparently went down the entire left side of his body to his hip. He was working with the forest fire services in the summer to pay for med school and he got caught in an old cabin.

"Don't worry. It didn't hit my necessary organ, or my liver for that matter," he said with a laugh. *Wow, this guy certainly seems to be taking it all in stride.*

He was a doctor in Toronto, specializing in skin grafting. Made sense. He was fun, rugged and really seemed happy. The night went on and we just kept talking and getting to know each other. Well, the ugly lights came on. My girlfriend was on the arm of a new suitor and it was time for this princess to go home.

"I'd love to take you for dinner tomorrow after the conference. May I?"

"Yes, you may," I said, as we exchanged phone numbers.

He walked me to the front, hailed a cab for me and then gave me a short powerful kiss. Kind of like a punch to the lips: *bam.* Not bad, not good, just bam. *Oh well, it was late. Let's see what the doctor comes up with tomorrow.*

We met at a lovely restaurant and he was the perfect gentleman. We talked more about his family and how they really wanted him to settle down and get married, but he was so focused on his work that he really wasn't dating much. He did say though that he was thinking of relocating back to BC and, because of his specialty, he was a wanted commodity.

"Oh, that's exciting. When will you decide if that's a possibility for you?" I asked.

"I already said it was a possibility. I just don't know whether I'm going to or not," he replied rather tersely.

Easy there buddy, I'm just making conversation here. I shifted in my seat. His bad attitude was not a good sign.

"So, how do you like Toronto then?" I asked. "Well clearly, I'm *not* liking it very much if I'm thinking of relocating."

Holy shit buddy, now this is too much.

"Listen, what just happened to the nice guy that I met yesterday? You're being very rude," I said.

"C'mon, why are you even out with me? Feel sorry for the disfigured guy who can't get a date?" "Not at all! You're a gorgeous man with beautiful eyes and smile and a strong muscular body and you happen to have a scar on your face from saving people's lives! I really thought you were a nice guy who had accepted what had happened and was moving on positively with your life."

"Whatever. Jill, this is a pity date. Why don't you just admit it?"

"Oh buddy, the only thing I pity is your piss-poor attitude," I said as I got up and left.

You know when they say some people have baggage? Hell, with this guy, there wasn't even any room for my carry-on. He had it all tied up.

Flight attendants, clear the cabin for take-off. This was going to be a solo flight for the dear doctor.

John #41

Gawd, have I even gotten through the year yet? Oh well, I did tell the universe that I was ready. It was time for another heart-to-heart. After some deep contemplation and self-realization (a.k.a wine time with my friend), I decided that I was still in this to win this. *Here we go again.*

He was another cutie from the gym: tall, blond, blue eyes and a rock-hard body. Not that I wanted to be known as *that* gym-girl—remember young hot lawyer John #36 from the same gym?—but, what the heck!

We had been flirting at the Smith machine for a couple of weeks; it was time to move in for the kill. I mean, it was time to go out with this lovely young man (another younger man, RAWR!). After all, he had seen me in my finest form with my hiney sticking out and my back arched, so he saw the possibilities. He is a male after all. Ya can't blame him.

We went for a casual dinner after a workout and he was very fun and boyish, but I was realizing that he was maybe a little *too* boyish. *How old was this guy anyways?* Funny thing was, we went to the same place I had gone to with John #36, I guess because of its proximity to the gym and the clean eating sushi thing.

Now, what would be the chances of it happening twice?

"Jill, you little minx. Aren't you a popular one?" said that annoying acquaintance that had said that stupid shit to the previous date. This time, though, we were sitting and she was just leaving.

"Oh, hey. I was just going to go to the restroom," I said as I got up to get rid of this bothersome human. "Oh, great to see you. Call me!" she said as I walked out of earshot. Some people, how do they tie their shoes on their own?

I got back to the table.

"What was that about?" John #41 asked.

"Oh some girl who doesn't have the art of conversation or proper social skills."

"Ooo, that's cold!" he said.

"Nope, just call it like I see it. She's not anyone close to me, nor do I ever want her to be. It's okay. Not everyone plays well together," I said.

"Fair enough. Hey, I really wanted to go for a tour around the park tonight. Skies are clear. It's mild out. What do you say?"

"Sure."

We got into his sporty little car and went for a spin into the park, stopping at "Lovers Lane", which wasn't really—just kind of a heavy petting and smooching area. The cops were always stopping full-on fornicators.

We actually got *out* of the car and went to look at the magical lights overlooking the water and the city. Now, you *know* I'm a sucker for a view. We were standing there taking all the magic in when he stepped behind me and put his strong arms around my body. *Mmm. This is promising.* As a matter of fact, I was starting to feel *his* promise in the small of my back. He turned me around and tried to take my lips in his. *Ewww.* This was not good. His tongue was flicking like a frog in a room of flies. I stepped back. "Whoa!" I said as he grabbed my arm as I almost went over the edge of the stairs.

"You okay?" he asked.

"Yeah, yeah, I'm good. Hey, it's kinda cold. Can we go please?"

"Oh sure. Sorry you're cold. You're such a hot tamale, I didn't think you'd ever get cold," he said.

After *that* kiss and *those* words, I was getting colder by the second.

We got back in the car and he went in again.

"No. Thanks, no," I said as I held up my hand. "I just don't feel the spark. Sorry, I don't think that we're compatible beyond friends," I finished.

"Really? You didn't like the kiss? Girls usually love that tongue move and you're not feeling it?" *Dear lawd son. I'm not sure if you've noticed, I'm a WOMAN, not a girl.*

"Uh, yeah, just not my thing I guess. If you wouldn't mind

dropping me off back at the gym and I'll grab my car thanks," I said.

Boys, boys, boys, if you're learning your kissing skills from a book and *girls* like it, lose it. A woman wants to be consumed like a moist, sumptuous peach, dripping her juices, devoured like a plate of oysters, sucked, slowly licked, teased. Not like take-out from McFlies.

JOHN #42

So, I've dated old, young, older and younger still. Time to shake this shit up. How's about someone closer to my age universe?

BAM.

I changed gyms and my selection of Johns was on a whole 'nother level. *Let the games begin anew gentlemen.*

"Excuse me, you seem to do some different exercises with these new pieces of equipment. Would you please give me a couple pointers?" said a very cute guy who certainly looked in my age circle.

"Sure. What are you looking to focus on?" I said.

"Mostly my shoulders, but I could see that you seemed to be working your chest, I think," he said.

"Oh, you were focused *there* were you?" I said playfully.

"Oh, god no, sorry. I must sound so creepy. No. I've never been much of a gym rat."

"Oh, so *now* you're calling me a gym rat?" I couldn't help myself.

"I'm going to start again. I'm John #42 and I've been so focused on my school then my career that I've never really focused on gym time," he said.

"Well, you look like you're in pretty good shape," I said.

"Well, I run and I'm pretty active outdoors when I take the time and I eat fairly clean, except for the wine."

He had me at wine. "I was just yanking ya. It's all good," I said, as I started to show him some exercises. *He smells so good, even for being in a gym. Damn.*

We kept talking in between our workout and he was proving to be a worthy opponent. Or, should that be ally?

I went to the gym the same time the next day and there he was. *Yes.*

"Hey Jill, nice to see you. You want to do some weights together?" he said, sounding so formal. "Sure!"

We started laughing, touching, bantering and having far too much fun for being at a gym. He asked me if I would like to go for dinner the next night.

"Sure, sounds good. You want to meet here or at the restaurant?" I asked.

"Oh, I'm kind of old fashioned that way. I would love to pick you up and treat you like the lady you are."

Oh, and treat you will, kind sir. "Okay, why don't we say that we go from here after I finish my workout?"

"Okay, sounds good. Looking forward to it, Jill," he said.

How fun! This guy has similar interests. Okay, so he wasn't a gym rat, but being fit was important to him AND he liked wine. So, let's do this!

The anticipation was driving me crazy! He just seemed so normal and nice and pretty sexy. What could go wrong?*

There I was, working out in my sexiest little workout gear ever. He was a half hour late. *No biggie.* I actually did say after *I* worked out, so maybe he'll just come when I'm usually done. *Maybe it was traffic, whatev...*

"Hi, are you Jill?" asked a rather large hulking man.

"Um, why do you ask?"

"Well, it's just my brother John #42...he's kind of been detained," he said.

"What do you mean? Is he in customs?" I asked.

"No, not really. He's uh. Well, he was caught shoplifting and also charged with assault."

"What the fu..."

"It's not his fault. He was doing something for me, but he wasn't supposed to do it like that."

"What the hell's going on?" I asked.

"Listen, he's a good guy, but we've had this competitive thing and he owed me, so he thought he'd repay like this," he said.

"Listen buddy, I don't know you or what the hell you're talking about."

"He'll be released tonight, but he won't be able to make it to dinner."

"Uh, well, you can tell him that he need not worry about it or ever speak to me again."

"But he's…"

"No, if what you're saying is true, then I have no use for someone like him in my life. If he has another story that isn't him being a criminal, then I'll at least hear him out. Otherwise, no," I said with surety. *Damn.*

He didn't have another story.

*(Mental note: never ask that question. You open the universe up to all sorts of shenanigans.)

John #43

I was just getting back from my run by my gym and was waiting for the light to cross the street.

"Hey, you work out there don't you?" asked a nice looking guy that looked somewhat familiar.

"Uh, yeah," I replied. *I know, I know, another fitness guy.*

"I just joined a couple months ago. I mostly run, but I'm trying to do more cross-training to avoid injuries. Oh sorry, this must seem terribly intrusive," he said.

He sounded like some kind of charming European, so I said, "Not intrusive at all. I just got back from a run myself. How far do you normally run, or do you run for time?" I asked.

"Oh, these legs stop at 40 minutes, no matter what. How about you?" "I usually go for an hour or a little bit more. I feel like I'm finally warmed up at half an hour," I said, as we crossed the street together.

We got up to the entrance and he said that he was just going to head for a run, then hit some weights. I was just going to do my weights then, so we said our goodbyes.

These "randomly on purpose" meetings kept happening all week until one day he was at the gym the same time as me to head out for a run.

"Hey, you want to run together today?" he asked.

"Sure," I said as I was sizing his long legs up. See, he was always in his suit when I saw him because he was coming into the gym as I was leaving, so I was pleasantly surprised to see his lithe, muscular legs.

I had never really run with a man of interest before. It was great! We had the same stride, he was a great conversationalist and he was really growing on me. Turns out he had lived in Germany for 10 years after he got his Masters in Psychology. He had a son, got divorced and then moved back to Canada four years ago. He was cute in a bit of a dorky way. He had blue eyes, dimples, glasses and curly hair and he didn't really fall into the metrosexual category *at all*. He was more of a non-descript dresser. Oh well, I could work with it.

"You're so easy to talk to and a great running partner. Thanks for the run and conversation," he said as we got back to the gym.

"Thanks. You're not too bad yourself," I replied as we stood in the entrance of the gym. Well, *this* was getting awkward. *Ask me out John #43. Don't turn out to be a dud.*

"You coming to the gym tomorrow?" he asked.

"Yup. I was going to do the step mill though, you know, to avoid those pesky injuries," I said, referring to his comments when we first met.

"Ah, good idea. I should too. Say, would you like to grab a bite after?"

"Sure. Where would you like to go?" I said thinking I needed to dress for the occasion.

"How about the new Korean fusion place?"

"Ooo, I haven't been there yet. Sounds good. I'll see you tomorrow," I said and, with a hop in my step, I turned to head to the change room.

We met at the gym the next day and I gotta tell you, I had some butterflies. This guy just seemed so different, and in a *good* way. He was very intelligent, well-travelled and schooled, and just so gosh darn cute.

The restaurant was within walking distance, so we strolled there and he offered me his arm. *So gentlemanly.* I was having one of those "oh-so-comfortable" moments, like I had known him for years. Dinner was delicious and he was continuing to charm the pants off...well, not quite yet, but hopefully we'd get there.

He walked me back to my car and asked what I was doing on the weekend. I told him that I was going to a wheel-a-thon to raise money for a charity at such-and-such track on Saturday and that he should pop by. He was visibly happy that I had asked him, but he said that he had his son's soccer game. He asked what time it went until and I really wasn't sure.

"All I know is that it starts at 10:00 am and then we keep wheeling around the track until we raise enough money via an online campaign."

"Would you like to go for a short run before you go to the event? I don't get my son until 10:00 am and you're literally going to be driving right past my place," he said.

"Sure! I was going to run anyways, so that'll be fun to have a partner for some company," I replied.

So we agreed that I would come to his place at 8:30 am, have a run, and then go to the event from there.

I showed up at his place in my finest sweating attire, a.k.a butt lifting tights and a booby baring bra top. His place was super cute. It was a protected heritage house, so that meant that it couldn't be torn down, only renovated internally. I was waiting in his foyer, but was seeing that he had done some really nice work on it so far. He had a little backyard with enough room to have an outdoor eating area and some space for bocce ball. Our run went swimmingly—or I guess it would be runningly, only that's not a word. Anyways, he was into me and I was into him. This might be the start of something really good. After our short run, he said that he would message me when his son's game was over and if I was still at the event, they would come by. He gave me a sweet kiss on the cheek and I left for the track.

It turned out that the event was going to be all day, which was a good thing because John #43 would be able to come by. He messaged me midafternoon saying that they had just finished up and would swing by to say hi. He also said that he had to drop his son back off before dinnertime to his ex. I had butterflies again. *Holy smokes, I'm going to meet his son already. Yikes. I don't even know if I'm ready for this.*

It was my turn to wheel around the track and, as I was coming around the far side of the track, there he was with his son. *Wow, a ready-made family. Just add water. Okay, maybe I'm getting ahead of myself here.* They both stood there and clapped for me as I went for my second round. *So sweet!* I was grinning ear to ear when, all of a sudden, I got bumped from behind. *What the hell? This isn't smash-up derby people.* I turned to see my girlfriend with a weird wild look in her eyes.

"Who are the cheerleaders you got there?" she asked.

"Oh, just a guy I met at the gym with his son," I said.

"And you didn't think to tell me?" she said, all miffed.

"Well, we only just met and I wanted to see where this was going to go first. He just happens to live close by and I invited him to come. Besides, it's all for charity. I'll see you on the other side sucka!" I said, as I peeled out—okay, as much as I could in an old hospital-issued wheelchair.

When I gave the chair to the next participant, I went over to where John #43 and his son were. His son was a pretty cute lil' guy and John #43 was just beaming. We chatted for a bit. He bought me a Powerade at the canteen—keeping me hydrated, you know—and then asked if I wanted to come by for dinner after. *Hmmm. Why the hell not?*

"Sure!" I was becoming used to saying that with this lovely man. We agreed on a time and I went back to cheer my team on.

It turned out that we were finished a little bit earlier than expected and I knew John #43 was dropping his son off about now. So, I thought I would just head over. Sometimes being spontaneous isn't the best decision, though, as I was soon to find out.

I got to his place, but he wasn't back yet and I *really* need to go potty. I had kinda needed to go when I left the track, but I thought that I could hold it. Well, not the best idea. I had gone to his backyard doing the "potty dance" and kept saying to myself that I was an adult. *I can hold it.* Only, I couldn't. *Shit!* I looked around and I couldn't see any of his neighbours, so I squatted in his hedge. Yup, a grown-ass woman havin' a pee in a man's hedge. Classy, I know. Thank goodness for the leaves, otherwise this would have been *completely* uncivilized.

"Hey Jill, how long have you been here?" John #43 said as he drove up five minutes later.

Whew, right? "Oh, not long. Whatcha got for dinner?"

"I thought we'd have a seafood spread with some prawns, scallops and mussels."

"Mmm," I said, as he opened the door.

"You want to be my sous chef?" he asked.

"Sure, I just need to wash my hands first," I said. See? Totally civilized.

We had a blast working in his kitchen together and then he set up the table outside for us to eat at. *Eww.* I was sitting right beside the "pee hedge". Now, I couldn't smell anything, but still. *Ewww.*

We talked and talked and then it was getting a bit cold out, so we went back into his house. It was such a nice cozy feeling, like love lived there. He seemed so balanced and nice and had a way of making me feel special. Well, he *was* a doctor of the mind, so it made sense that he would understand communication. He got up to fill my wine glass and when he came back, he took my face in his hands and kissed me. It was so sweet and gentle. He sat back down in the chair across from me, though. *Hmm.* "What's wrong?" he asked.

"Oh, well, that kiss was nice and I guess I'd just like a little more, that's all," I said throwing caution to the wind.

"Oh, wow, that's so refreshing that you're so honest. That's highly unusual. Truth be told, I find you very attractive and I really want to consume you right now. But I want to take it slow with you. I haven't really dated since the divorce because no one has ever seemed worthwhile and with you it's just different. With having my son too, it makes it challenging."

"Well, that's kind of funny because you've already introduced me to him, if you're wanting to take it slow..." I responded.

"Yeah, I know. It just felt right and the event was a good cause and it's good for him to be a part of all aspects of my life."

"Okay, fair enough," I said, a little pouty because I really wanted some more kissing action.

The rest of the night was still really fun and he did come over to the couch after a little while for a little more sugar. Don't they *always* come for more?

"G'night Jill. This was the most fun I've had in years. Thanks for opening my eyes to new things. When can I see you again?"

"Well, I'll be at the gym Monday and Wednesday and I have plans on Friday and Sunday but nothing *yet* for Saturday."

"Splendid! How would you like to go to a contemporary ballet with me on Saturday?"

"Sure!"

"Okay, I've got some late patients Monday so I will likely see you Wednesday at the gym. Is it okay if I call you during the week?"

"Sure!"

Mental note, get a thesaurus, to change up my "sure".

He called me a taxi and we shared a pretty steamy kiss in the foyer before it got there. I was weak in the knees. *Beep. Shit, taxi's here.* Off I went and I was on cloud nine.

I got a call on Monday night after the gym from John #43 and we were bantering up a storm. We talked about the rest of the weekend and how our respective days were. He called again Tuesday night and it was wonderful. *I could get used to this. No games.* He was calling because he wanted to, being an adult. *Oh how refreshing!*

Wednesday came and a client came in from out of town. They wanted me to meet their new partner over dinner, so I obliged and went with them. John #43 called like clockwork and I actually excused myself from the table to take the call and let him know that plans had changed. We spoke briefly and he said that he would call me the next night.

Our calls were something that I looked forward to and it was so nice to know that I would get a call from him every night. He had asked if I would like to go for a run Saturday morning, shower up at his place, hit an art show, and then change and go to the ballet.

"Sure!" Clearly I still hadn't purchased a thesaurus.

I got to his place on Saturday morning and we headed out for our run. *Wow, this might be turning into something.* He wasn't that sensual with me *yet,* so that was a bit of a concern, I knew he wanted to take it slow but on the flip side he was so easy going, so cute, so fast. *Holy crap.* He had dialed up his click and I was straining to keep up. Maybe I should start concentrating a little more. We went over some old train tracks and then there were the tall cement medians all along the sidewalk. With his long legs he hurdled right over the cement barrier. I got to it and put my left foot up on it to step over, but my other foot slipped on the loose gravel as I was propelling forward and my body basically took a free fall from the top of the barrier. I landed right on my hip on the hard pavement. *Thud.*

I just laid there. I had never felt so much pain in my entire life. John #43 had turned around just in time to see me land.

"Holy shit Jill. Are you okay?"

"No. I'm not. Ouch. This hurts so much. I can't move my leg." Neither of us had brought our cell phones and we were about a mile away from his place. "Would you please go get your car and drive me to Emergency?"

"Shit. Are you sure? You're so calm. Do you want an ambulance?"

"No, it'll be much faster if you just run to your house and then take me. Would you please help me to the grass first? That would suck if I got run over too," I said with a weak smile. *Damn, it hurt so much!* He got me over to the patch of grass and ran to get his car.

In Emergency the doctor started poking around. "Ouch!" I said, as I swung my fist around to try and connect with his face.

"Oh, does that hurt?" the moronic doctor asked.

I now had tears in my eyes because of the pain. "Yes, it hurts a lot," I said quietly.

It turned out after the x-ray that I had a hairline fracture in my hip. Yeah, I don't cry over nuthin', ya know.

We got back to his place and he said he wanted to cancel the ballet. "No! I still want to go. I'll just have to walk with the cane they gave me," I said. I was all hopped up on medication and I thought it might be kinda Madonna-sexy with a little black dress and a cane.

Well, let me tell you, it wasn't sexy. I just looked like I couldn't walk in my high heels and I had a very odd walking prop. Sometimes vanity just isn't worth it. But the night wasn't a total loss. The ballet was inspiring and I had never seen such athleticism.

He dropped me off at my place and helped me in. There was

really no point in asking him in because the medication was starting to wear off and my hip was throbbing. He kissed me goodnight and said that he would call the next day.

I kept to myself for the week, nursing my hip and looking forward to our conversations every night. He was good to talk to, but there was no flirting like I need. *Hmmm, maybe with more time.* We planned to have dinner at his place on the weekend and he came to pick me up with his son and his sons' friend. He said that he just had to drop them off first and then we'd have dins.

For some reason, I wasn't having it. I guess I was cranky because of my hip or something, but I just wasn't digging the smell of Big Macs and adolescent boys and I wasn't sure if I ever would.

We dropped them off, got back to his place, and my crank wasn't getting any better. I was pretty much pouting, but trying to will myself to change. Nope, it wasn't going to happen.

"Look, I don't know what's wrong, but all of the sudden, I'm just not into 'this'," I said circling my hands.

"What do you mean?" he asked.

"I guess I'm not used to little boys or something, but I'm not the right person for you."

"But I don't understand. What went wrong? We've been having such great conversations and our kisses have been magical," he tried.

I guess *that's* what it was too. He was so nice and a great conversationalist, but there was no real consistent magic. I just saw a life of mediocrity with a white picket fence and sharing the Saturday morning paper. *Dullsville.*

"I'm sorry. I just don't feel the raw sexual spark that I need. I'll just go home, thanks," I said, as I got up and gave him a friendly hug.

In this scenario a "bird in the hand wasn't worth two in the bush". Although, *his* bush came in *mighty* handy for a pee!

JOHN #44

He was another man with kids, but they were all grown. He had no contact with his ex, had no roommates, was part of the family business, had a large Dutch family that he was close to, was a non-religious Christian, said he was 5 feet 10 inches (which is just my lower height limit), lived on the waterfront...*okay, stop right there. Hello John #44.* We met at a casual place and I was more dressed down than normal in my jeans and flat boots, but hey, I had been walking to a lot of dates lately and I needed some foot comfort for once!

He was a little nervous, along with being a little high strung and a little shorter than the 5 feet 10 inches on his profile. *Maybe he forgot his lifts and had a lot of coffee today.* There was a little boy cuteness to him and, although he was ten years older than me, he didn't miss a beat in our conversation. It went well and we decided on date two. I feel like this is Sesame Street: date one, then after that comes date two, and if he's lucky, date three!

He asked if I would please come out to his place and we'd go to a new French restaurant on the water. He had a couple private guest rooms with locks (for my comfort and safety) and he would like me to stay over. We would go for a run on the beach the following morning. That sounded reasonable…

…until I got to his place for the date. I was dressed in my usual "one-level-down-from-a-hooker" and rang his bell.

"Hey! Wow, you look amazing!" he said as he hugged me and brought me into the foyer. He started staring at my shoes, which was kinda unsettling. *Does this guy have a foot fetish?*

"Is something wrong?" I asked.

"No, no, not really. It's just…are you going to wear those shoes?"

Are you kidding me? "Uh, yeah, AND this dress AND this coat," I spewed out.

"Oh crap, I'm sorry. It's just you're so tall."

"Well, you knew that when you met me. A tall woman who wears high heels becomes taller. It's magic!" I said, still defiant.

"Oh man, I'm so sorry. I shouldn't let my minor insecurities get in the way. Here I am with the most beautiful woman who also happens to be tall. How did I get so lucky?" I wanted to and should have walked right out where I came in, but nooo, I didn't.

"Look, if this is going to be an ongoing issue, this isn't going to work," I said.

"It was my momentary lapse in judgment. Please Jill, it won't happen again. You look amazing and your shoes are beautiful and I really appreciate you putting in the effort to dress up and come all the way out to see me."

"Okay, but the moment a hint of this comes up again, I'm out," I told him.

"You got it."

Dinner went really well. We were laughing and he shared stories of his three grown daughters and how proud he was of them. He was excited about the family Christmas at the Springs this year. Christmas was only one week away and he was kinda beating around the bush about my plans and then hinted that maybe I could come up for the day.

"Whoa, slow down cowboy! You're still not sure if you can handle my high heels! Let's just take it one day at a time," I said, a little freaked.

We got back to his place. He stayed true to his word and had my room all set up for me. We said goodnight and he gave me a kiss on the cheek. Remember, he was a non-religious Christian, but clearly still had some rules. I got into my room and, just in case, I scanned the room for cameras. You never know, especially with these Christian types. I slept like a log, woke up, turned my phone back on and saw three messages from him. *Well, isn't someone an eager little beaver.* I splashed my face, brushed my fangs and headed upstairs to see what the little guy was doing.

"Hello, you sweet angel!"

Wow, I don't think anyone but old Auntie Joe ever called me that.

"You said you don't eat before you run. What do you say we go for a run, wash up and I'll take you for some breakie?"

"Um do you have any coffee first please?" I asked, still shaking off the vino from the previous night.

"Yes! Yes, of course!" he said as he scurried over to the coffee pot.

"Let's enjoy the view for a bit," he said, as he led me outside to the breathtaking ocean view. *Wow, I could get used to this.* I finished cup two and we headed down to the beach for our run.

You know how everyone has a different style of running? Well, let's just say John #44 was more than a little spastic. He asked me how long I normally ran for and when I replied, "An hour at least," his face dropped. Was I okay with only going for 20 minutes today? Well, what other choice did I have? He stopped abruptly about ten minutes in.

"What's wrong?" I asked, thinking he might be having a jammer.

He tried to plant a kiss and missed and it was sadly awkward. *Let's hope that there will be no more of that nonsense during this short cardio excursion. I'm trying to keep my heart rate up!* We finished up our tiny marathon and headed back to get cleaned up. He still maintained being a perfect gentleman as we went to our separate wings of the house and we regrouped upstairs when I was ready.

On the way to the restaurant he seemed *really* fidgety, like, way more than I'd seen him be so far. We pulled into the parking lot and as I was getting out of the car: "Daddy!" a young woman yelled as she came running over and hugged him.

Wow, that's coincidental, running into one of his daughters here.

"Jill, this is Maggie," he said, as she came over and put her little paws on me in a bear hug. It was more of a cub hug really. She was such a tiny little thing.

"It is so fun to finally meet you! Daddy showed me your pictures and told me all about you!" she said a little too excitedly.

What the hell was with these guys? And exactly what pictures did he share? My online dating ones? I was feeling very uncomfortable.

She ran up ahead while he stammered, "Uh, I was meaning to tell you. We're meeting my family for breakfast."

"Seriously? I just met you! I know I'm really easy going, but I don't know if I'm comfortable with this," I said.

"Well, you just met Maggie and the rest are just like her."

"What do you mean the rest? Is there a whole commune or is it just your daughters?"

"Um, no. My mom and dad, um, and sisters and their husbands and their kids."

What the hell? I was speechless. I felt like I was being brought in as an offering to the Dutch gods of Pannekoek.

There were 24 family members there. 24! I was being pawed at by all of these little Dutch people with questions being peppered at me from all angles. I was in the land of the Lilliputians. "Mom", as she wanted me to call her, was very sweet, though, and she saw that this was all a little bit much. She pulled me aside and said that John #44 hadn't gone on a date with anyone for almost two years because he didn't want to waste his time on women who weren't exactly what he was looking for. *I wonder if he told her about the high heel situation?*

"Mom" ordered mimosas all around and I could see that this was a matriarchal situation. Funny too, because it became her and I—ruling the roost seated at the head of all the tables. Lunch turned out to be quite fun actually, but more in the "adopt-a-new-family kind of way" than anything romantic.

After lunch I knew what I had to do. It was brutal. I wanted to be with him just for his family. They were all so wonderful, but there just wasn't a spark with this little guy, John #44. He was devastated as I told him on the drive to his place to get my car. Hey, you can't fake it people. Or, I guess you can, but I just couldn't.

Goodbye "Mom". I'll miss you. Sniffle, sniffle.

John #45

Our eyes locked across the bales of hay. Really, I can't make this stuff up people. I had gone to a country party with a girlfriend and, along with some bales of hay, the hoe-down was set in an old barn. It was put on by a group of undercover cops. Now, I don't know how successful they were at staying undercover if this was already a known fact to all of the pedestrians that were there. Maybe they usually wore disguises. Anyways, it was pretty fun just letting loose with a bunch of people in a down-home kinda way.

I had just come from the bar with my mason jar of wine and there he was: a silver fox with steely blue eyes and a gorgeous smile. You could tell that he had gone grey early, and it totally suited him. I went over to where my girlfriend was and the fox came right up to me.

"You are absolutely stunning! I wasn't expecting a beauty queen to appear between the bales of hay," he said, as my knees buckled.

"That's very sweet of you to say. I'm Jill."

"Terribly sorry. I'm John #45 and it's my distinct pleasure to meet you. Are you having a good time?"

"Yeah, the people here are lots of fun. I guess they love the opportunity to blow off steam from being undercover. Are you undercover too?"

"Well, aren't you the little P.I.? It wasn't supposed to get out to the guests who didn't know us. Oh well, cover's blown now," he said with a laugh.

"Oh, sorry. I thought if I knew, then it was common knowledge to everyone else."

"No worries, would you like to dance?" he said as he grabbed my hand and we went to the dance floor.

So much fun! We twirled and laughed and then slow danced. I felt like I was a teenager dancing with the most popular guy in school. It was so romantic. We ended up going outside and sitting on a bench and stargazing. *If this is the simple life that some people talk about, count me in!*

He had his arm around me and, as we were talking, he leaned in for the sweetest most sensual kiss. Yeah, the kissing bandit was at it again! We kept kissing and it was getting so steamy and wonderful and—"Jill, I really need to be going now," my friend said as she approached us.

"Oh, okay," I said as I fumbled around to pick up my purse from the ground.

"I could drive you home if you'd like," John #45 offered.

You could drive me to the junkyard, you smoldering hunk of man, I was thinking, but said, "That's okay. It's best that I keep my friend company back into the big city."

"I'd really like to see you again. May I have your number?"

And my panties. "Sure," I said as I gave him my number.

We kissed goodbye and I got in the car with my friend.

He called the next day and our conversation flowed. We made plans to meet up the following day, which was a Monday. He was going to be in the area that I was working in, so we would meet there and then grab a bite, if ya know what I mean! Hubba hubba! He ended up showing up early and came into the office. I was a bit flustered. You know when you have the exact plan all played out in your mind and then kablooey! You have no control over the situation. I was so wrapped up in me being uncomfortable that I didn't notice he was a little quiet and withdrawn until he asked if we could sit on a park bench and talk first. *Here we go again.*

"So, here's the thing. I like you so much and I couldn't even imagine a better connection for just meeting someone. My ex-wife, well, technically we're not officially divorced yet, but she's got cancer. We've been separated for two years and have been somewhat amicable because of our teenage son. Anyways, she just told me about it yesterday and all of memories we made together came rushing back. It's not like I feel in love with her still, but there is this bond that I can't ignore. I've asked her to move back so that our son and I can take care of her through this time. Jill, I can't even begin to say how sickened I am with this. I thought that I had finally met someone that I could really start again with." "Wow, that is heavy. Hmmm. Well, you have to do what you feel is right and I can't even imagine being in your position," I said as I looked into his beautiful eyes that were welled up with tears.

Well shit. How could I be upset when, in the scheme of things, I was the healthy one and still with a world of possibilities? But still, shit.

John #46

"I love to travel! I feel like travelling is the best education and you really get to know who you are when you are out of your normal settings," said the new man of my travel dreams.

"I couldn't agree more John #46. I love to travel and I always seek out new experiences too."

He told me that he had retired early and he'd been blessed because he was able to live quite comfortably and take the time off to pursue his travels.

We agreed to meet. Even though this guy was about 16 years older than me, I figured he had to know how to treat a lady. *So, what have I got to lose?* We got to the restaurant at the same time and he was ANOTHER SHORTY! Stop lying fellas. Eventually we ladies will find out! He turned out to be quite funny in a self-depreciating way and the laughter kept flowing. I knew he was new to the site because he had told me, so I asked him how it was going. He told me that he hid his profile.

"What? Why?" I asked.

"Because I met you and I only want to focus on one person.

Life is so distracting that I think we need to put the brakes on sometimes and live in the moment."

Whoa, good answer buddy, but you're also putting a lot of pressure on this date.

The more he kept talking, the more he reminded me of someone. I wondered who...*hmm...oh shit! Regis Philbin! Oh no.* Now I couldn't get that voice out of my head and I started giggling. The lack of food and the over serving of wine wasn't helping either. My eyes were welling up. *Poor Regis.* I couldn't even breathe to tell him what I was laughing at, but how could I even *tell* him? I clearly found it hysterical, but he might be mortified. I finally settled my giggles down and we just pretended like nothing happened. The guy was just so sweet, though, so when he asked me on another date, I said yes. *What the heck? Hey, Kathie Lee would approve!*

We talked for most of the week and he found out that my birthday was coming up. I might have hinted ever so subtly. He said that he wanted to get me something and that it didn't matter that we had both just met. *Awww, diamonds, diamonds, diamonds.*

"You don't have to," I said.

I met him at his place and when I buzzed his penthouse he asked if I wanted to come up and have a little snack. I told him I'd rather save my appetite for the restaurant. Besides, don't we have reservations? We taxied to the restaurant. He was very excited about our dinner and said that it was for an early birthday celebration. He also said that he was so happy he could celebrate with me.

It was one of those highbrow places that have been around since forever and they had the best steak in the city. As you know, I loves my meat! He was acting a bit strange, but really, what's new? Everyone seems to have a bit of crazy in them and with some it comes out sooner than later. I perused the wine list and asked him what looked good to him.

"Anything under 20 dollars!" he said with a nervous laugh.

Well honey, there ain't even a glass *of wine here for under 20 bucks and you chose the place.* I suggested a moderately priced bottle that I knew was delicious and then he asked me, "Are you going to get an appetizer or maybe you should just have the steak?"

Was he trying to control what I was going to order? Nuh-uh buddy. "I'm not sure yet," I replied, as I picked up the menu again.

I don't usually have appetizers but him not wanting me to have one was making me want one for some reason. The server came back.

"I'll have the garlic prawns to start and then the bone-in rib steak rare please," I said as I looked at John #46 and smiled.

"I'll just have the filet thank you," he said.

"So what did you get up to today?" I asked him.

"Well, birthday girl, I spent the better part of the day getting your birthday presents."

"Really? That is so sweet of you," I said, wondering where the goods were. *Were they in his jacket? Maybe his pocket? It must be some small and very sparkly gifts if I couldn't see them.* I was getting excited!

"You're probably wondering where they are?"

"Um, no. Not really," I lied.

"They're back at my place, so you'll have to come up for a night cap to get them!" he said with a laugh.

"Huh, bribery eh?" I said with my eyebrow raised.

"No, not at all. I just figured you haven't seen my place yet and the view is spectacular and it would be nice to show you."

Hmm, maybe that's why he wanted me to come up before, not just to save money on an appetizer. We carried on with dinner and we got quite a few odd looks, maybe because I WAS SITTING WITH REGIS PHILBIN or a poor chap who had a screaming resemblance to him. We finished up and the taxi came to whisk us away to his abode. I agreed to come up for a "night cap" or diamonds, whatever.

His penthouse really was spectacular; he had a gorgeous south-western view of the ocean and the sunset. He asked me to sit down as he poured me a glass of wine and then went into the other room and said, "Close your eyes," as he brought in my presents.

"Can I open my eyes now?" I asked.

"Yes!" he said as he presented me with a wooden container the size of a boot box.

Hmmm, okay.

"It's wine! I knew that you liked wine and I got you some really fun ones."

"Oh, wow, well thank you. That's so nice of you," I said somewhat perplexed.

"There are three in there and they're a Marilyn Monroe theme."

"I see," I said as I opened the box. *Okay, this is actually an appropriate gift for just meeting someone, but with all the talk about lavish presents and spoiling me, I guess I just figured I would get something, oh, I don't know, sparkly.*

So I settled into my glass and we made some small talk and he seemed to get nervous again. *Sheesh, what is it with these guys?* He said that he had something to tell me.

I said, "We haven't even kissed yet, so you can't be cheating on me!"

He didn't really laugh. "This is really hard for me and I'm so sorry I wasn't up front with you." *Shit, is he a drug dealer or something?*

"It's just, well, I'm older than I told you," he said as he handed me his driver's license.

My mouth fell open. "Are you kidding me? You're 15 years older than you said you were, which now makes you about 30 years older than me, dude. I knew you were older than me and I rolled with it. But now *this*? And you lying about it?" All I could picture was me rolling this old guy in a wheelchair and cutting up his steak for him. Not my idea of fun.

Now some would ask the question: how could I not have known? Listen, the guy said that he was middle age and he looked like he had lived those years, but he was certainly not an old wrinkly guy. "Have you had work done?" I asked.

"Yes, I've had a couple face-lifts starting when I was in my early forties and I get frequent liquid lifts and fillers too."

Shit. This guy did not look like he was in his seventies, but then again, neither does Cher. Go figure. Mental note: get the name of his plastic surgeon for the future.

But now back to the business at hand.

"I can't do this John #46. That's a pretty big lie and I know you did it because you didn't want to be judged on your age. I'm not judging. I just don't want to be with someone who could be my father. Not my thing," I said as I got up to leave.

"Jill, I really wish you'd change your mind. At the very least, please take your wine."

"Alright then," I said, as I got up with my wine and thought, this was way easier to let him down this way, with this age reason as my out. I knew we weren't going to make a couple, but dreaded telling the little fella because he had been so nice until the *lie.* Dun, dun, dunnnnnn.

No thanks gramps. Last thing I need is for you to have a jammer while we're doing the wild thing, especially if I'm not in your will. At that age you're gonna have to pay to play old man...

VALENTINE'S DAY

"Guurl, why you wastin' that itty bity little party dress on me? You make me wanna RuPaul you!" squealed my gay friend Danny as I got to his place before our Valentine's date.

"Oh, sugar, I'm gonna make you wanna change teams with these boobies bouncing they way they are!" I retorted.

We did our 'kiss kiss' and then settled into our game plan for the evening.

Our love strategy was in full swing when I got a text:

"Happy Valentines Day Beautiful! XO."

Well, *this* was awkward.

"Who is this please?"

"John."

Oh, *that* narrowed it down.

Back to the strategy. So we were going to go to the upscale Blue Water Cafe, sit at the bar and look oh-so-fabulous and not like the desperate love seekers that we were. There *had* to be other singles that were out there for both of our sakes! We got a seat at the bar where we could rate—I mean see—everyone who came in. It's amazing how many apparent first dates happen on this most holy day of coupledom.

Danny and I started our commentary.

"Oh honey, if you can't walk in your bedroom in those stilettos, don't even *think* about walking out of the house with them."

"Wow, she really squeezed herself into that piece of material. Is that, gasp, neoprene?" we shuddered.

Ooo, what have we here? Mister, mister. Our eyes locked. It was intense. But, wait a minute, now it was offside because that woman beside him was apparently with him. He took her coat as he continued to stare. She turned to him, oblivious to all of this, and planted a wet one on his cheek. The host came and ushered them to their table. He motioned for her to go ahead of him so he could continue this game of eye lock. It *is* all about the game, isn't it? I broke our eye contact with an eye roll and turned to the bartender.

"I'd love another wine please." *Yeah, sure it's flattering that someone is attracted to me, but to what end? If a man I dated was doing that, I'd kick him to the curb, I'll tell you that right now.*

"What was that all about?" Danny asked.

"What?" I replied.

"That guy was so into you and you rolled your eyes at him."

"He's clearly with someone and that's not cool. What if that was my date doing that?" I asked. "What if they're like us? Maybe *she's* gay. They might just be friends, or even related, who knows?"

Huh, he may have a point. But, what was I gonna do? Go up

to their table and ask what their relationship status was? No. I still thought he was a he-hoe.

We ended up making fast friends with the gay posse that had saddled up to the bar and we had a blast. Turns out they were all in the restaurant industry, so we got whatever they had and all on the house. Who says love has to be between just two people when there's love to be found in new friends and glorious wine?

Although my lady bits were being sorely neglected...

JOHN #47

So, *he* was the John that had sent me the Valentines text. So sweet! I had upgraded my phone and lost some numbers, so when I clarified it was him, I was really excited. We had talked twice on the phone before Valentine's Day and he seemed like a solid guy AND he was Italian. He was 6 feet 2 inches tall, slim, with dark hair and deliciously dark brown eyes—my "Italian Stallion".

After my gay-date with Danny had ended, I had texted him back and he called me. I told him all about my night with my lovely friend. He was really easy to talk to and was very interested in everything I had to say. He was actually really listening—imagine that! We agreed to meet the next night.

It was a dark and stormy night *and* the day after Valentine's. Ominous. I had agreed to meet him for coffee, which I didn't usually do on an evening date, but he said it wasn't that he didn't trust me, but he had a few flakes and wanted a more casual meet first. I knew where he was coming from, so with *this* John, that was okay by me.

I drove around the corner of the coffee shop to park and, as I got out of my car, I saw him sitting there and I got butterflies.

I opened up my umbrella, which promptly flew inside out with the wind and almost lifted me off the ground. *What the hell? I'm not Mary Poppins.* After I wrestled with my umbrella, I ducked under the awning and as I was approaching the door, John #47 got up and opened it for me! It was love at first sight when our eyes met. We embraced and as I felt his body against mine, it was a perfect fit. I had never really believed in *love at first sight* before but I truly knew in my heart that I was going to fall in love with this man. I just had this feeling. This guy was so sweet, so manly, smart, handsome, tall, funny, attentive and just so gosh-darn sexy.

We talked and talked and then, when the staff was sweeping and putting the chairs up on the tables, he said, "Well, if *that* isn't the sign of an awesome first date, I don't know what is. We just shut down a coffee shop." I didn't want this date to end, ever! This guy was so amazing in every way; he truly was the man of my dreams. I had opened myself up to love and had kissed many, many frogs. Okay, too many to count but I was committed to finding true abiding love after all.

He asked if he could walk me to my car and as soon as we got outside the wind was insane. The rain was coming down in sheets. I knew it was useless to even try my umbrella again, but I didn't need to. John #47 took his coat off and held it over my head. Now this was the stuff of movies.

We stopped in the middle of the road and kissed and his strong body felt so right, like it was made just for me. He was so passionate and masculine and his raw scent was drawing me in, so when he asked me what I was doing the next night I said, "Having dinner with you."

We've been together ever since. When you know, you know. Love rules!

By the way, his name really *is* John…but he doesn't know the details about all the other Johns. Let's keep those tidbits as our little secret. ;o)

Ten Bits of Advice On Why He Might Not Be Quite Right For You

1. He's a "Catfish" and things don't *quite* add up when you meet him. Remember, if something smells fishy, it *is* fishy. (Side note: remember to pee after sex, 'cause fishy lady bits aren't sexy.)

2. If a man says he's going through a divorce or is "separated", demand to see the paper work. If he's legit, he shouldn't mind. Ask for his address because you want to send him a card or something. If he won't give it, there's a red flag right there. Whatever it takes, find out his real status before you get that "bitch from hell" calling you at all hours of the night.

3. When a guy says he doesn't have a problem with your height, your popularity, your wine consumption, or any other obvious thing about you, he's lying. He does. Run—don't walk—far, far, away.

4. If he mentions his ex in an overly caring way, it's a red flag. "It's for the kids." Bullshit. He still has a connection with her. Don't be fooled. Step away. You don't need to be the Canadian version of *Sister Brides*.

5. If he's late for your first date, no. Just no. Think about it. He's not late for other important events is he? *You're* important. Has he ever been late for a flight and missed it? Well, if the loser has, you don't want to be with him anyways. You're welcome.

6. Pro hockey players, unless you get them before they make it big—just stay away. Not worth the time. Even if you do "score" one, what, or more importantly *who,* do you think he's doing on his road trips?

7. Not all effeminate men are gay, but when your "gay-dar" is telling you he's gay, it's right. If you want a sexless relationship, just get married.

8. Not all men can handle being a "Pillow Pal". Do your screening. If he's too clingy and needs affirmation, kick him to the curb.

9. Nice guys don't finish last. They need to stop their whining and up their game. If *you* want a nice guy, fine. Me? I want a nice guy alright, but also someone who will devour me sexually and not be afraid to have some tongue play and dirty talk.

10. Men and women *can't* be friends. Now before you get all, "Oh, my best friend Mike is so sweet and awe-some. He'd *never* step over the line," he's thinking right now about how he's going to bone you.

UNTIL NEXT TIME...

I hope that you had as much fun reading my book as I did writing it!

Connect with me on social:

FB: JillSinclairAuthor
TW: @Jill_Sinclair
IG: @msjillsinclair
Peri: @Jill_Sinclair